THEMATIC CATALOG OF THE
WORKS OF
JOHANNES BRAHMS

Da Capo Press Music Reprint Series

GENERAL EDITOR: FREDERICK FREEDMAN

Vassar College

The N. Simrock

THEMATIC CATALOG OF THE WORKS OF JOHANNES BRAHMS

[Thematisches Verzeichniss sämmtlicher im Druck erschienenen Werke von Johannes Brahms]

New Introduction, including Addenda and Corrigenda
By Donald M. McCorkle
University of British Columbia

DA CAPO PRESS · NEW YORK · 1973

Library of Congress Cataloging in Publication Data

Simrock, N., firm, Berlin.

The N. Simrock Thematic catalog of the works of
Johannes Brahms.

(Da Capo Press music reprint series)
Reprint of the 1897 ed., in German.
Bibliography: p.
1. Brahms, Johannes, 1833-1897—Thematic catalogs.
ML134.B8A35   1973   016.78'092'4   72-5954
ISBN 0-306-70271-1

This Da Capo Press edition of *Thematic Catalog of
the Works of Johannes Brahms* is an unabridged republication
of *Thematisches Verzeichniss sämmtlicher im Druck
erschienenen Werke von Johannes Brahms*, originally
published by the firm of N. Simrock in Berlin in 1897.
It includes new introductory material prepared especially
for this edition by Donald M. McCorkle.

Contents

Acknowledgments

Research for this study and for my own progressing catalog of the extant manuscripts of Brahms has been carried on primarily in Washington, Vienna, and Hamburg. Because it has required considerable time to be spent in Europe over a period of five years and an immense amount of cooperation to get at the original sources, I would be remiss if I did not express my deep appreciation to people and institutions whose aid has been most helpful. I first became aware of the dearth of documentary studies relating to Brahms bibliography—particularly concerned with questions of authenticity and accuracy—while teaching a graduate seminar at the University of Maryland in 1964. To my astonishment I realized that one could not readily determine whether a music edition of any of the reputable publishers of Brahms' works *necessarily* conveyed the musical text as approved by the composer. This is not to suggest that most of the editions are incorrect, but only that so many changes were made (and numerous errors were left uncorrected) in reissues and new editions after Brahms' death that one is compelled to make careful comparisons to determine which details are accurate, and which are not. To make comparisons of musical text one normally turns to a thematic catalog for guidance in selecting the variant editions. But what does one do when he discovers that no wholly accurate catalog is available—when several catalogs exist which differ from each other in important details? In my case, this discovery has led me to probe the state of the catalogs to establish a standard for further documentary studies.

The Graduate School of the University of Maryland contributed to a summer abroad through a faculty award. Professor Oswald Jonas (University of California at Riverside) shared some of his knowledge of Brahms sources as well as some valuable leads for locating a few of the more transient manuscripts. Professor Karl Geiringer (University of California at Santa Barbara) gave encouragement and information to fill gaps in the sources he had known so well in the Gesellschaft der Musikfreunde in Vienna before World War II.

In Vienna, I am deeply indebted to Frau Dr. Hedwig Mitringer (Gesellschaft der Musikfreunde), Hofrat Professor Dr. Leopold Nowak (Osterreichisches National-bibliothek), and Professor Dr. Friedrich Racek (Wiener Stadtbibliothek). In Hamburg, the unfailing courtesy of Dr. Kurt W. A. Richter and his assistant Helga Heim (Staats- und Universitätsbibliothek) cannot be adequately acknowledged. Six other people in Europe have been particularly helpful: Kurt Hofmann (Hamburg), Universitäts-Dozent Dr. Rudolf Flotzinger (Vienna), Christa Landon

(Vienna), Dr. Elfrieda Prillinger (Gmunden, Austria), and Hans Schneider (Tutzing).

In the United States, I am always in the debt of my friends in the Music Divisions of The Library of Congress and the Library & Museum of the Performing Arts (The New York Public Library), as well as to the staff of The Pierpont Morgan Library (New York), and to Professor Otto E. Albrecht (Philadelphia). My colleague Professor Eugene Helm (University of Maryland) has favored me with his critical ears and eyes often in the course of this research. And certainly my thanks go to Professor Frederick Freedman (Vassar College), the General Editor of the Da Capo music series, whose recognition of the need for this reprint made the publication possible. Through his courtesy, the Vassar College copy of the Brahms *Verzeichniss* was used as camera copy for this reprint.

To my wife, Margit, I am grateful for intellectual support, for walking the Austrian and German *Gassen, Strassen, und Promenaden* in search of Brahmsiana, and for exquisite readings of Brahms at the piano, which makes bibliographic research worth all the trouble.

DONALD M. McCORKLE

Vienna, April 1971.

INTRODUCTION: *The Simrock Brahms Verzeichniss*

The second issue of the *Thematisches Verzeichniss sämmtlicher im Druck erschienenen Werke von Johannes Brahms,* published by the firm of N. Simrock in 1897, is to this day the most nearly accurate and reliable thematic catalog devoted to the compositions of Johannes Brahms (1833-1897). It is, at the same time, long out of print and extremely rare today, for the reason that it was superseded by later issues in 1902, 1903, 1904, and 1910. Strictly considered, these subsequent issues were not actually new editions, if we understand a new edition to require new printing plates, but new impressions, or "title and plate editions" (*Titelauflagen* and *Plattenauflagen*), in which minor alterations were made in the title pages and some few major as well as minor alterations were made in the plates for the body of the catalog, including the supplementary catalogs and indexes. The designations *Neue Ausgabe* (New Issue) and *Neue vermehrte Ausgabe* (New Enlarged Issue), which were added to the title pages of the third/fourth and fifth/sixth issues, respectively, do not actually mean that improvements have been made; indeed, the converse is more likely the situation. For, beginning with the third issue (1902), the essential material remains fundamentally the same, but the quality of accuracy and authenticity, not to mention typographical clarity, progressively deteriorates, for reasons to be explained below.

The first edition, thus the first issue, which appeared in 1887 as the *Thematisches Verzeichniss der bisher im Druck erschienenen Werke,* etc. (Thematic Catalog of the Existing Published Works...), was complete only to 1887, that is, through Opus 101 and eight Works without Opus Number. For the second issue, the content was slightly revised and considerably expanded by alteration of plates and addition of some forty-one new plates to accommodate the newer works composed from around 1886 to Brahms' death in 1897. The title was accordingly altered to "Thematic Catalog of the Collected Published Works of Johannes Brahms," for in fact all the works which Brahms had considered worthy of publication, and had been published during his lifetime, were accounted for in this second issue. The resulting rather modest catalog, to which we may refer as *SBV II,* consisted of two preliminary leaves and 175 folio pages, and measured, bound, about 28.5 x 19 x 1.5

cm. All later issues were physically the same, except for the internal alterations which were "mended-in" unobtrusively.

While *SBV II* is no longer representative of the most scholarly plan for a composer's thematic catalog, and lacking though it is in some important particulars, it is nevertheless very useful because of its relatively precise and complete data about essential matters without which one cannot progress further in studying a composer's work. Qualifications are important here. The *Simrock Brahms Verzeichniss* was prepared as a compromise between a publisher's promotional and sales catalog and a composer's catalog. As such, it is neither as complete nor as accurate as the modern scholar, musicographer, librarian, or musician would ideally wish it to be. It does contain for each composition published through 1897 full identification of the work, the imprint and collation of the original edition, the thematic incipits, and a list of supplementary specifications, performing materials, and arrangements. Three supplementary catalogs and/or indexes classify the works in several summary orders. However, the catalog does not contain historical data, such as places and dates of compositions and first performances, listings of posthumous editions, locations and collations of autographs, annotations, references to pertinent literature. The bibliographer will regret that slant-lines, brackets, and other descriptive devices which would have made identification of particular issues easier were not included. The most serious deficiency of all is the lack of any sort of introductory statement to describe the plan, function, and use of the catalog.

But within the prescribed limitations, and implemented by the present edition's New Introduction, including Addenda and Corrigenda, *SBV II* can well continue to serve as a valuable reference work until the time that a truly comprehensive thematic catalog can be produced.[1]

It may seem curious that for Brahms there is still nothing comparable to the monumental thematic catalogs of Mozart, Beethoven, Bach, and Schubert, among others. An attempt to compile such a catalog was made around 1933, during the Brahms-centennial flood of publications, by one Alfred von Ehrmann. Issued as a supplementary volume for his biography, *Johannes Brahms: Weg, Werk und Welt* (Leipzig: Breitkopf & Härtel, 1933), Ehrmann's catalog, *Johannes Brahms, Thematisches Verzeichnis seiner Werke*, was inevitably more up-to-date than Simrock's in accounting for the posthumous editions (most of them, not all), composition dates, first performances, location of autographs (prior to World War II), and references to the *Sämtliche Werke* (*Gesamtausgabe*) editions. But because of an evident haste in compilation, dominant among various shortcom-

---

[1]The present writer has such a comprehensive catalog of the works in preparation. It is anticipated that it will include for the first time a detailed analysis of all the editions and extant Mss. (See also footnote 18.)

ings, it is highly inaccurate throughout, and is probably best consigned to the oblivion that has overcome it in recent years.[2]

There already has been a reprint of sorts of the *SBV*, prepared as a *Thematic Catalog of the Collected Works of Brahms*, edited with foreword by Joseph Braunstein ([New York]: Ars Musica Press, [1956]). This is essentially a selective photographic reprint of one of the later issues and of supplementary material from several other sources. The editor's statement that it is "a revision and enlargement of the fourth edition of 1907"[3] in itself raises several serious questions of authenticity, because: (1) there was no fourth edition (*Auflage*) *per se* of *SBV*, though there was an undesignated fourth issue (*Ausgabe*), published, however, in 1903; (2) no other reference to a 1907 issue has been found by the present writer; (3) the "revision" was mainly a process of eliminating material, whereby the collation data for the original editions and the statement of supplementary specifications, materials, and arrangements, other than Brahms' own, were deleted before reprinting the catalog; (4) the enlargement consists entirely of titles and incipits, with a slight bit of chronological data, for posthumous editions. All of the latter was photographically borrowed, without notice or acknowledgment, mostly from Ehrmann's *Thematisches Verzeichnis*. For the imprints of original editions in

---

[2]The thematic material is derived from the *Gesamtausgabe*, rather than the original editions, and so has advantages over the *SBV* for those who have more concern with the critical editions of Mandyczewski and Gál. The historical and descriptive data, on the other hand, are so flawed by factual errors that the user must be cautioned against reliance on this information. Moreover, the imprints and collations are incomplete, and the lists of supplementary specifications and arrangements are not included; thus the bibliographer is left without essential documentation. To rectify some of these problems Breitkopf & Härtel issued an *Anhang* in 1952. This little-known and extremely rare pamphlet corrects some of the many serious errors; but it does not correct enough to justify very much respect for Ehrmann's *Thematisches Verzeichnis*.

Alfred von Ehrmann, whose identity is now obscure, evidently was a well-known Viennese poet and writer about music, as well as sometime staff member of the *Wiener Zeitung* (the Austrian state newspaper), until his death in 1938. He was descended from an old Salzburg family, but he himself lived in Baden near Vienna. According to R. H. Schauffler (*The Unknown Brahms*, New York, 1933, 21-22), who became acquainted with him ca. 1929, he was also an amateur violist. I have been unable to discover any more published biographical information than the small amount which appears in two notices of a memorial program given in Vienna on October 5, 1948 by his son, Richard Ehrmann. The notices, for which I am indebted to Frau Dr. Hedwig Mitringer, appeared in *Die Presse*, Jahrgang III/39 (Sept. 25, 1948) and *Wiener Zeitung* Jahrg. 241/235 (Oct. 7, 1948).

[3]In the Foreword by Joseph Braunstein. However, in subsequent correspondence, Dr. Braunstein has intimated that his editorial relationship with the Ars Musica Press reprint was considerably less than decisive, and that in fact his work with the project began after the mechanical procedure was already in operation. The editorial policy and production were directed by David Grunes (Omega Music Company, New York), who apparently aimed at eliminating as much of the original Simrock appearance as possible, beyond retaining the bare essentials of the *SBV*. Dr. Braunstein is unable to confirm the date of the issue used as camera copy by the printer, or whether he himself ever saw the "1907" date (letter to the author, November 1, 1970). The author thereafter made several attempts to contact the publisher for clarification but was unsuccessful in getting a response.

the identification headings, the too-often incorrect information printed in the issues of *SBV* following 1902 is retained without comment. In the second part of the catalog, a newly set and expanded "Classified Index" replaces the original systematic catalog. The alphabetical index has been retained with a supplementary list, but the original appendix summarizing the arrangements and transcriptions and concluding with a name and subject index has been eliminated. None of these alterations has been noted or explained. All things considered, therefore, this work amounts to a particularly misrepresentative and misleading catalog, which is, accordingly, the least adequate thematic catalog of Brahms' works.

The original *SBV II* is not altogether a bibliographer's dream, as has been implied already, and without adequate explanation and guidance it can easily become a researcher's nightmare. The German title itself is unintentionally somewhat misleading, for though it does not actually say so, it may imply that it is the catalog of all the works of Brahms. Rather, in the cataloging fashion current among music publishers during the late nineteenth century, it claims only to be a catalog of the *collected published* works. So, withal, the title must be understood to mean that only those compositions which already had been published in composer's original editions and in authorized arrangements and transcriptions through the year of Brahms' death are included in *SBV II*. It can be concluded that Brahms did not deem certain other works worthy of permanent notice in a catalog. Although it was prepared by his principal publisher, Fritz Simrock for his firm (N. Simrock), it is a composer's catalog, since all of his editions with other competitive publishers are properly included. The subsequent issues, published after the passing of both Brahms and Simrock (1837–1901), became increasingly further removed from verity and more exasperating, as the volume of newer and simplified versions, arrangements, and transcriptions of Brahms' works swelled to subordinate and often to obscure the standard editions. A more detailed explanation of this incredible situation follows below. But first, a brief history of the *Simrock Brahms Verzeichniss* that should clarify some important matters of perspective.

The Historical Context
Evolution of the Catalog

That this catalog ever came into being is in itself a remarkable and fascinating tale of affection, persuasion, and contention. The protagonists in what was clearly an intensely dramatic conflict over matters of principle were Fritz Simrock and Eduard Hanslick (1825–1904), the preeminent Viennese music critic and the master's close friend and champion. The antagonist seems to have been Johannes Brahms himself.

As the Brahms biographer Max Kalbeck remembered the scenario in 1903,[4] Simrock approached Brahms some time prior to 1885 and proposed that a thematic catalog be published coincidentally with the completion of Opus 100. His avowed purpose was twofold: to supply a publisher's catalog of Brahms' works which would accelerate the promotion of his music and editions before the public, and to offer a reliable reference book for the musical scholar. He apparently had the best intentions of making the work as fine and copious a catalog as could be compiled, under the editorship of his staff editor, Robert Keller. The projected result would presumably have been a model catalog, meeting the needs of the scholar as well as the trade.

Rather characteristically, Brahms remained openly non-committal about the scheme but passively opposed it until the moment of truth began to press upon him. As the predetermined opus number was reached, he vigorously and vehemently, and not a little sarcastically, opposed the project on grounds of propriety. Basically, he felt that living composers should not presume to be so honored because the world would look upon it as vanity. As Kalbeck tells it, Brahms wrote to Simrock, on June 16, 1885, as follows:

> Indeed, I find the entire affair absurd and unnecessary, but, nevertheless, I can speak so much the less against it, since there are, of course, two catalogs already. I would find it certainly more sensible if you were satisfied to publish a catalog of the "recommended works!" That would be such a little, pretty, and cheap advertisement for Senff and Fritzsch! An anthology of poems and poets of my choice would also be elegant! But now, so that I may also say something positive: I am thoroughly opposed to the "historical data" which you and Herr Keller have in mind. I find them not only unnecessary, but also impertinent. It seems disgracefully vain, in my opinion, and furthermore, no one will believe, that I do not assist with it and even properly cannot.

> Therefore, leave them out by all means. And then the notion that the catalog shall come out with Op. 100 goes very much against my grain. That would seem to be a jubilee; and you will also, further, come to the realization that no such occasion exists. So let it come out earlier, in connection with the next one or two *opera*, which perhaps I will still find in old drawers. Because, surely you do not believe, do you, that I, a well-to-do man, continue to work?

[4]Max Kalbeck, *Johannes Brahms*, 3rd ed., 4 vols. in 8. (Berlin: Deutsche Brahms-Gesellschaft m. b. H., 1912–1914), IV/1, 89–94.
The exact date, September 4, 1884 appears in a letter from Fritz Simrock to Brahms in Mürzzuschlag (Austria), in which he mentions his intention to issue the thematic catalog and inquires whether Brahms has any objections. (See Kurt Stephenson, ed. *Johannes Brahms und Fritz Simrock; Weg einer Freundschaft, Briefe des Verlegers an den Komponisten* [Hamburg: J. J. Augustin, 1961], 197.) Brahms responded four days later. (See Max Kalbeck, ed. *Johannes Brahms Briefe an P. J. Simrock und Fritz Simrock*, 4 vols. [Berlin: Deutsche Brahms-Gesellschaft m. b. H., 1917–1919], III, 70.)

You may perhaps show this note to Friend Hanslick, and let him tell you
that I am right....[5]

Ultimately, he acquiesced, but with such restrictive conditions as to severely
diminish the ultimate value and completeness of the catalog as projected by
Simrock. His stipulations that there should be no "historical data" (by which
Hanslick surmised that Brahms understood biographical details, in particular
the identification of women who had inspired certain works, and dates and places
of composition), no annotations, and no observance of Opus 100 as an anniversary
obviously made it difficult for Simrock and Keller to produce a comprehensive
catalog. Brahms, again characteristically, had his way. The important historical
and biographical data one looks for in a fine catalog were scrapped. He did
indeed figuratively look into his "old drawers" (*Alten Schubladen*) and slipped
in the Opus 101 Trio, in addition to Opus 100, to dispel the inevitable acclaim
which would be forthcoming after a jubilee composition. Moreover, he prevented the preparation of a portrait which would grace the book as frontispiece.
Simrock assiduously sought to have him captured by a portrait painter in Switzerland during a holiday; but Brahms just as assiduously avoided the painter by
avoiding Switzerland, and thus prevented his image from being graven, or as Kalbeck delightfully puts it, "from having the nose stolen secretly from him out of
his face."[6]

Hanslick's role in the proceedings was clearly that of supporter of Simrock and
coaxer of Brahms in promoting the project. His exhortations to the master of the
need for correct information in thematic catalogs—which he said he found want-
ing in the Mendelssohn and Schumann catalogs[7]—apparently did the trick, when
combined with his plea: "You should not want to hold him [Simrock] back—
contemporaries and posterity beg you not to."[8] When the first edition finally
appeared in 1887, the distinguished critic, with his usual perspicacity, lucidity,
and tact, was able to prophesy in the pages of the Vienna *Neue Freie Presse* that
the world might yet expect much of Brahms, and "certainly the second part [that
is, beginning with Opus 102] of the Thematic Catalog will not commence less
lovely than the first has ended."[9]

---

[5]Translated from Kalbeck, op. cit., IV/1, 90–91. For the explanations of two obscure allusions
in his letter, the following suggestions can be offered: (a) The two catalogs were probably the
unidentified "Verzeichnis 1875 u. 1883, zwei Hefte," recorded in the *Nachlass* inventory (see
footnote 13); (b) Simrock evidently advertised his "recommended works" in the music pe-
riodicals of both Bartholf Senff and E. W. Fritzsch.

[6]Kalbeck, op. cit., IV/1, 93.

[7]By which we presume he meant the *Thematisches Verzeichniss der im Druck erschienenen
Compositionen von F. Mendelssohn Bartholdy* (Leipzig: Breitkopf & Härtel, 1846–1853, 1873,
1882) and the *Thematisches Verzeichnis sämmtlicher im Druck erschienenen Werke R. Schumanns* (Leipzig: Schubert, [1860, 1863, 1868]).

[8]Kalbeck, op. cit., IV/1, 91.

[9]Kalbeck, ibid., IV/1, 94. The substance of the newspaper feature article by Hanslick is included as a chapter in Eduard Hanslick, *Musikalisches und Litterarisches* (Der "Modernen
Oper" V. Theil) [Berlin: Allgemeiner Verein für Deutsche Literatur, 1889], 131-141.

Brahms did not help with the project, nor, we are told by Kalbeck, would he have been able to do so, even if he had been capable of overcoming his self-consciousness, for "he was," in the biographer's estimation, "the last to give reliable information of his works and his life."[10] We, of course, are in no position to dispute Kalbeck's assessment of his close friend's memory, but one can reach somewhat different conclusions from the same documentary evidence he adduces. In particular, he cites two so-called "memoranda calendars" (*Notizkalendern*) kept by Brahms as evidence of memory lapses and unreliability. The first, a fourteen-leaf book in which six leaves contain his own autograph entries of opus numbers, titles, publishers, publication dates, composition places and dates, and honoraria received for most of the works, extends from Opus 1 to Opus 79 (i.e., 1851–1879).[11] While Kalbeck doubted its value because of its gaps and termination at 1879, the present writer finds the data therein to be largely accurate and verifiable. However, only the sketchiest of data are noted for many of the solo vocal works, which may well be an interesting palpable illustration of his zeal for secrecy in the biographical circumstances of vocal composition. The second, an unidentified and presently unlocated index, was summarily dismissed by Kalbeck as being unreliable as historical evidence, apparently on the weakness of one example. In that example, according to Kalbeck, Brahms had listed four songs, a choral piece, three sonatas, and a trio as being composed in August of 1886, a production which the biographer rightly believed to be too much for a single month, and nearly too much for an entire summer. But we may be inclined to suggest—as Kalbeck himself obliquely observed, apparently without catching the significance of the observation—that the explanation lies in Brahms' creative process; namely, that he *completed* the composition of all nine works in the one month, following several months of gestation. So, this hardly seems a fair basis for doubting Brahms' chronological memory.

We do not know whether or not Brahms participated actively in the preparation of the *SBV*, nor do we know whether he took particular notice of its existence.[12] The formal *Nachlass* inventory reveals that a copy of the first issue was in his library when the collection was indexed following his death,[13] but the copy could

---

[10]Kalbeck, ibid., IV/1, 92.

[11]Vienna, Wiener Stadtbibliothek, J. Nr. 32886 N, no title. It was transcribed and analyzed by Alfred Orel in "Ein eigenhändiges Werkverzeichnis von Brahms," *Die Musik* XXIX/8 (May 1937), 529–41.

[12]However, his comment to Clara Schumann in a letter of May 1887 certainly conveys a confirmation of his antipathy to it: "Simrock has just published a catalogue of my works. If he should send a copy to you I need hardly tell you that I did not ask him to do so. On the contrary, I prevented it as long as possible. I could not, however, forbid it." (See Berthold Litzmann, ed., *Letters of Clara Schumann and Johannes Brahms*, 2 vols. (London: Longmans, Green & Co., 1927), II, 112.

[13]The "Nachlass Inventar," prepared under legal jurisdiction, exists in at least two copies: Gesellschaft der Musikfreunde (Vienna) and Staats- und Universitätsbibliothek (Hamburg). (Microfilm copy of the latter in the author's collection.)

not be located recently in the Brahms collection of the Gesellschaft der Musikfreunde in Vienna (which owns most of his personal library), or in any of the
other likely collections in Austria or Germany. Certainly, the absence from the
inventory of *SBV II* further confirms the probable posthumous publication date.
Fortunately, two important copies of *SBV I* somewhat related to Brahms are
extant and are valuable sources for corrections and some other historical details.
These are Eusebius Mandyczewski's (Gesellschaft der Musikfreunde) and Max
Kalbeck's exemplars (Library of Congress), both of them bound with the 1897
supplementary pages. Dr. Mandyczewski's copy contains marginal notes relating
to occasional errors in the catalog, some composition and first performance dates,
identification of pre-1929 owners of numerous autographs,[14] and miscellaneous
details. Inasmuch as Mandyczewski's notes seem clearly the result of his own
sleuthing and deductions, it must be supposed that he did not get his information
from Brahms. Kalbeck, always the digging researcher, concentrated on tracing
sources of tunes and isolating motivic derivations and exchanges within Brahms'
compositions, as well as correcting some chronological errors. It is not likely that
Brahms would have helped him with this sort of data.

The Authoritative Publishers of Brahms
Brahms and Simrock

The venerable firm of N. Simrock has long been virtually synonymous with the
music of Brahms. This was particularly true until the expiration of copyright in
1927, and had been so since Fritz Simrock and Brahms established a friendship
remarkably close for a publisher and his principal composer. N. Simrock could
rightly claim an authoritative relationship with Brahms until the late 1920's,
when the *Johannes Brahms Sämtliche Werke* was issued (1926–1928) by Breitkopf & Härtel with the Gesellschaft der Musikfreunde, Brahms' music had fallen
to the public domain, and the Simrock firm was sold to Anton J. Benjamin in
Leipzig. This authoritativeness does not necessarily carry over, and the authority
certainly does not, to the modern firm, revived in 1951, of "N. Simrock, London-
Hamburg," which is a trade name for the London firm of Alfred Lengnick &
Company, a former agent for the original house.

Fritz Simrock, a contemporary of Brahms, inherited the firm from his father,
Peter Joseph, who had had the foresight to add Brahms to the catalog at around
1860, thanks to Breitkopf & Härtel's unresponsiveness after their initial Brahms

---

[14]Ehrmann evidently saw these notes and extracted the names of autograph owners for inclusion
in his own *Verzeichnis* in 1933, without further verification that Mandyczewski's identification
of owners was still valid after the many intervening years.

ventures. N. Simrock had acquired, since the founding years of Nicolaus in 1790, such composers as Haydn, Beethoven, Weber, Mendelssohn, Schumann, and Hiller. During the flourishing reign of Fritz, 1868–1901, the firm moved to Berlin —by 1870, the German political and cultural capital—and added Dvořák, Bruch, and Johann Strauss to its catalog, with Brahms at the center. It was to Brahms' considerable advantage, obviously, to be the foremost composer in the catalog of the leading conservative house in Europe, as it was to Simrock's advantage to promote the music most agreeable to his own taste.

As Kurt Plessing has said of Fritz: "Simrock was a man! He was a man with all the good human qualities, with human defects and human weaknesses."[15] Fritz genuinely appreciated Brahms' music and Brahms himself, so it is a matter of curiosity that his treatment of the composer was inconsistent. From the very interesting correspondence between them[16] it is clear that Simrock was inordinately solicitous and even jealous of Brahms' well-being. So solicitous was he that he undertook all manner of responsibilities upon himself to relieve his friend of mundane concerns, such as, for example, the handling of money, both income (including investment) and expenditure. While his publishing relationship with Brahms was relatively generous, he persisted in the ancient and outmoded tradition of paying the composer one-time honoraria instead of adopting the modern plan of continuous royalties for each work—but Brahms named the honoraria, and haggled intensely!

He was moved by a compulsion—a neurotic compulsion has been intimated by Kurt Stephenson[17]—to be the exclusive publisher for the man he cherished, but he was continually denied complete success because of Brahms' lack of enthusiasm for such a restrictive arrangement. Certainly, Fritz had to suffer much discomfort and inconvenience from the composer's obstinate and mercurial temperament during the long friendship. His particular desire to produce a *Gesamtausgabe* after 1888 was frustrated by Brahms, who thought it was a senseless idea, and by his own parsimoniousness. In order to proceed, it was necessary for him to acquire rights to his competitors' editions, especially those issued before 1868, and to persuade Brahms not to send any more works to other publishers. He was able to acquire the Breitkopf rights (and editions), but through fault of his own he did not consummate negotiations with C. F. Peters and C. A. Spina (Vienna). Brahms finally put an end to the covetousness by insisting that friendship was above business, and that he could publish with whomever he chose. Through all of this, and the other supposed pecuniary and personal affronts which Brahms con-

---

[15]Kurt Plessing, "Fritz Simrock, aus einem gleichnamigen Lebensbild," *N. Simrock Jahrbuch* III (1930–1934), 17.

[16]The correspondence appears in two publications; see footnote 4.

[17]Kurt Stephenson, op. cit., 3–14.

tinually groused about, he nevertheless maintained great affection for Simrock as publisher and friend for nearly four decades.

But probably the single most important question in their relationship is that of Simrock's integrity and care in printing precisely what Brahms wrote on his manuscripts. This question is being subjected to thorough consideration in forthcoming studies,[18] but it can be said here briefly that the original standard editions and piano arrangements by Brahms published before 1902 certainly carry the complete authority of Brahms, engraving errors notwithstanding, because of the strong convictions of Fritz Simrock, the meticulousness of Brahms, and the skill of the house editor, Robert Keller. But both publisher and composer rather too often allowed errors to be committed to print, and hence to posterity, through occasionally careless proofreading, or, on Simrock's part, by obfuscation. (During the administration of his successors it becomes uncertain whether a line separates obfuscation and outright fraudulent intent.) On the part of Brahms, three vexations were most apparent: he often protested against what he regarded as slipshod proofreading by Keller, the excessive number of arrangements published without consideration of his feelings (especially arrangements by Keller, whom he considered a "Philistine"), and Simrock's evident commercialism in having foreign translations prepared for some of his songs and other vocal works. (Some of the other publishers were, therefore, likewise not above reproach.)

The professional competence and range of responsibility of Keller is another important question to be considered, for he was the editor of the Brahms compositions from about 1878, if not earlier, arranger of no fewer than sixty piano reductions and arrangements of Brahms' major works from 1873 to at least 1890, and editor and compiler of the *SBV* of 1887 and presumably of 1897. In fact his name and handiwork are as ubiquitous in Simrock's Brahms publications as his identity is elusive. Perhaps Brahms was right in classing him among the undistinguished and unimaginative hacks. And yet it is clear that he was the chief technician in the firm, and, therefore, the person most responsible for what we have before us.[19] Very little is known about him, and some of that is contradictory. He was characterized by Kalbeck (1903) as "Simrock's musical adviser, arranger, and proof-

---

[18]The present author is currently pursuing some of the fundamental questions of authenticity in preparation for several projected comprehensive studies and documents of a bibliographic and critical nature on Brahms' creative process. At this time (1970), nearly all of the extant Mss have been cataloged and scrutinized for visual evidence of compositional elaboration and editorial revision. Another stage of the research is a comparative analysis of the autographs and original editions to determine which presentations of the musical texts can be considered definitive. Some indications of the complexity of the problem of establishing authenticity of Brahms sources were presented in a paper (unpublished), "The Other Versions of Brahms," read at the Annual Meeting of the American Musicological Society, New Haven, December 27, 1968.

[19]But he is not mentioned by Walther Ottendorff-Simrock, who wrote the Simrock entry for *Die Musik in Geschichte und Gegenwart*, 14 vols. (Kassel: Bärenreiter, 1949–69), XII, Cols. 722–25.

reader, a useful and capable man moreover;"[20] and again (1917) as "the industrious, capable arranger and editor [of the] Brahms compositions and publications and also compiler of the thematic catalogs of 1887 and 1910."[21] If he did indeed edit the 1910 revision, then one wonders where he was in the intervening years, and why his name does not appear on arrangements after 1890. Otto Erich Deutsch, as usual, may have the correct if rather astonishing answer in the context of his appraisal of the 1902 revision of the Brahms Catalog: "The utility of the work of Robert Keller, the anonymous editor of the thematic catalogue (*who died before Brahms* [my italics]), is thus diminished by reason of the vested interest—or, rather, the vanity—of the publishing house."[22]

After 1901, very consequential musical and bibliographic changes were effected in the treatment of Brahms' compositions. Hans (Johann Baptist) Simrock, nephew of Fritz, reorganized the firm as a stock company, opened branches in Leipzig, London, Paris, and New York, and proceeded to proliferate his holdings of Brahms. This was effected by reissuing the original editions in a variety of guises, and by increasing the production of newly created variant versions of Brahms—all of this to accommodate the widest possible audience by the most diverse (and often inappropriate) media. These editions proliferated to such an extent that today one cannot hold much confidence in those issues bearing the corporate imprint of "N. Simrock, G.m.b.H., Berlin." For within these issues are the more-or-less exact reissues (as undesignated "title and plate editions") of the genuine original editions, done by lithographic transfer—which may or may not contain alterations not by Brahms. These usually are labelled *"Original Ausgabe"* (see explanation on page xxvii), and are further identified by the names of other publishers used for distribution abroad, such as Stanley Lucas, Weber & Co. (London), Schott & Co. (London), Alfred Lengnick & Co. (London), C. F. Peters (Leipzig), and G. Schirmer (New York). An identical situation obtains for the so-called *Original Ausgaben* issued in the cheaply printed series of *Simrock's Volksausgabe*. But the really serious concern is in the numerous post-1897 arrangements and transcriptions which more often than not did not and could not have had the authority of the composer, and which the firm apparently promoted strongly as authentic Brahms. Moreover, Hans Simrock further consolidated his

---

[20]Kalbeck, op. cit., IV/1, 90.

[21]Max Kalbeck, ed. *Johannes Brahms Briefe an P. J. Simrock und Fritz Simrock*, I, 107.

[22]Otto Erich Deutsch, "The First Editions of Brahms," *The Music Review* I/2 (May 1940), 125. This extremely valuable two-part (May and August 1940 issues) bibliographic article by the late Viennese musicographer is virtually unknown today, even though it is probably the most significant research yet published on the original editions. As far as is known by Frau Christa Landon, his student and executrix of his literary estate, Professor Deutsch did not revise his bibliography after it was published in 1940. Nor, indeed, was she aware that he had published this study or had done any research on Brahms. The present writer is profoundly indebted to his work, which presents much of the otherwise unavailable documentation needed for pursuing advanced bibliographic research in Brahmsiana.

Brahms holdings by absorbing in 1907 the firm of Bartholf Senff, which brought him all rights to their four original editions. (None of these later issues are listed in *SBV II*, of course, and thus are of no particular concern to the user of the catalog, but an understanding of the situation is important for the bibliographer and musician who may innocently regard them as unquestionably authentic texts.)

A random example should illustrate the implications of the total bibliographic problem. Breitkopf & Härtel, the original publisher of the *Sonate*, Op. 1, issued the first edition in 1853. They subsequently printed two more issues from the original plates, with no apparent alterations other than on title pages. A fourth issue was a transfer. A second *edition* was then included in a collection of *Pianoforte-Werke zu zwei Händen* (1875). When Simrock acquired the rights to the *Sonate* he published the third edition, as revised by Brahms, in 1888. How confounding, then, to conclude from *SBV II* that the Breitkopf third or fourth issue (not so designated) of the original edition and the second edition were the two prints available in 1897. (Evidently Simrock did not add his own third edition to the catalog!) But the extreme and unconscionable, if legal, step was taken next: In the ensuing issues of the *SBV* the Breitkopf editions are deleted altogether, N. Simrock is cited as the publisher of the original edition (1853!), and the collation refers to the third edition (not so designated). Moreover, an arrangement for four hands by Paul Klengel has been added as the optional edition.[23] (The ultimate stage in this type of bibliographic deception which negates the authenticity of many of these later posthumous issues is too often a further obfuscation. Once the scruples were lowered and the copyrights expired, numerous pirated reprints were issued by other publishers who apparently removed the name of the arranger or transcriber from his work, thus implying that the edition was pure Brahms. Perhaps even Klengel's name at some time was omitted from *his* arrangement of Opus 1.)

Why, we must ask, did the Simrock successors—not only Hans, but also Richard Chrzescinski, who led the firm through a devastating era (1910–1923), and finally Fritz Auckenthaler, the grandson of Fritz Simrock, who, until he disposed of the firm in 1929, had commissioned numerous other musicians to "revise" thirty-five of Brahms' works to compete with the Breitkopf & Härtel *Sämtliche Werke*[24]—why did they permit such corruptions of Brahms' intentions, while simultaneously working magnanimously to perpetuate his memory? The changes in the four issues of *SBV* published between 1902 and 1910 are symbolic reflections of the entire situation. Perhaps, Erich H. Müller gives us the key to the pre-

---

[23]Details of bibliographic differences among the various issues, such as illustrated in this paragraph, can be deduced only by a careful reading of Deutsch in conjunction with the entries in *SBV*; they cannot be found clearly spelled out in *SBV*.

[24]Deutsch, op. cit., 124. Reference is to the Simrock firm and not to Auckenthaler.

vailing reasoning when he pinpoints the essence of Hans Simrock's tenure at the head of the firm:

> But his principal work was devoted to the legacy of Brahms. It was motivated not only out of purely commercial interest, but, on the contrary, even more from the sense of improving and perfecting the deceased Master. Thus, Hans Simrock was concerned with price reduction and publication of single issues and transcriptions to effect the propagation of Brahms' art in wider circles. But, above all, he with a number of admirers of the great Master began the "Deutsche Brahmsgesellschaft G. m. b. H.," which published, in addition to the Brahms correspondence . . . the great Brahms biography by Max Kalbeck, the Joachim biography by Andreas Moser, and various other valuable works of Brahms literature.[25]

And so one witnesses the well-intentioned reversal of the musical and spiritual legacy of Brahms, whose creative years were spent refining and polishing his works until further revision was unreasonable before granting his *imprimatur*. What irony for a person who took comfort in the faith of *I. Corinthians* that "the dead shall be raised incorruptible." Far from being granted security as hallowed works of the dead, his legacy was to suffer corruption "in a moment, in the twinkling of an eye, at the last trump,"[26] by his most responsible descendants.

And what of the other responsible descendants?

The Other Publishers

Before Simrock obtained a virtual Brahms monopoly around 1868, Brahms published with Breitkopf & Härtel (1853–1864) and J. Rieter-Biedermann (1858–1873), and intermittently with Bartholf Senff (1853–1854), C. A. Spina (1864), A. Cranz (1868), and G. H. Wigand (1854). After Breitkopf lost interest in him in 1864, Brahms sent most of his music to Rieter-Biedermann, and a few pieces to the other smaller firms. At various times in later years he returned to Senff and Cranz, and also started new publications with E. W. Fritzsch, C. F. Peters, and W. Spemann.

It has already been observed that Simrock bought the rights to the early works originally published by Breitkopf & Härtel, and in due course republished them under the Simrock imprint. Without a detailed comparative analysis of each item, one can only speculate that revisions in the musical text which may be found in the Simrock reissues represent the revised thinking of Brahms. Under the circumstances, however, a healthy amount of skepticism would seem to be warranted.

---

[25]Erich H. Müller, "Zur Geschichte des Hauses Simrock," *N. Simrock Jahrbuch* I (1928), 19–20.
[26]Cf. *Ein deutsches Requiem*, Sixth Movement.

Next to Simrock, certainly, Rieter-Biedermann was the most important propagator of Brahms. The firm was established by Melchior Rieter-Biedermann in Winterthur in 1849. A branch was opened in Leipzig in 1862, and this eventually superseded the Swiss office. Melchior became Brahms' principal publisher in 1861 when Breitkopf rejected the *Piano Concerto*, Op. 15. His enthusiasm for and friendship with Brahms brought both of them rich rewards, for until his death in 1876 he produced a total of twenty-two major works. Among them were such triumphs as *Ein deutsches Requiem*, the *Magelone Romanzen*, the *F Minor Piano Quintet*, the *Paganini Variations*, the *Waltzes*, Op. 39, and numerous outstanding vocal works. It is important to note that his original editions of Brahms evidently remained inviolate during the Simrock monopoly and passed on, unrevised, to C. F. Peters when they bought the Rieter-Beidermann house in 1917. But not all of the Rieter publications are authentic: The catalog pamphlet issued by the firm in 1905 contains many additional *Bearbeitungen* undoubtedly made after Brahms' death.

Peters, for many years one of Europe's great houses, was only a minor publisher of Brahms, with but five *opera* between 1874 and 1892, until Heinrich Hinrichsen acquired the Rieter-Biedermann catalog, and they began to reissue the original editions of Rieter in *Edition Peters* jackets. After 1928, when copyright had expired, Peters became a major purveyor of Brahms by publishing also *Die neuen Brahms-Ausgaben der Edition Peters*, which were new editions of standard versions.[27] For this task, Peters solicited the editorial services of concert-artists and composers, notably Emil von Sauer, George Schumann, the Gewandhaus-Quartett, Julius Klengel, Karl Klingler, Carl Flesch, Artur Schnabel, Kurt Soldan, and Edgar Wollgandt. In this effort, the authoritativeness of Peters was dissipated by the incorporation of editions of doubtful value into a distinguished catalog simply to exploit the Brahms market. At the same time, Peters entered the race against Simrock and Breitkopf to establish a separate series of Brahms editions. It must have been pandemonium, in truth, to follow these three great firms in a commercial stampede to capture the market for Brahms. (Today, the New York house has eliminated the spuriosities and retains the original Rieter-Peters editions and some new editions; whether the European branches have done likewise is not known to the author.)

The Gesamtausgabe

With this background of corruption being perpetrated against Brahms' works by Simrock during the final years of copyright, and by Peters immediately after, it is no wonder that his devoted young friends undertook to produce a definitive

---

[27] A publisher's catalog, *Johannes Brahms, Verzeichnis seiner Werke, mit Einführung von Adolf Aber*, was issued ca. 1928 for the publications of C. F. Peters.

Gesamtausgabe for publication simultaneously with expiration of copyright. And it is hardly surprising that Breitkopf & Härtel collaborated. Eusebius Mandyczewski (1857–1929), the superbly capable musicologist and archivist of the Gesellschaft der Musikfreunde, who had been a close personal and intellectual friend of Brahms for many years, assumed the general editorship, and engaged as collaborator Hans Gál, his and Guido Adler's former student at the University of Vienna.

The result was the *Johannes Brahms Sämtliche Werke*, in twenty-six volumes, published by Breitkopf & Härtel for the Gesellschaft in 1926–28. Although the collected edition does not contain all of Brahms' works—most of his piano arrangements as well as the post-1929 discoveries are not included—it does contain probably the closest approximations that can be achieved in realizing definitive texts for the standard versions. The quality of the editing seems to be very accurate throughout, and the editors evidently compared all original sources available to them, in particular Brahms' own exemplars of the original editions and many of his autographs. It is apparent, however, that they did not consult some of the most important autographs, those printer's copies owned by the Simrock firm. (One suspects that, for obvious reasons, the Simrocks withheld these extremely revealing manuscripts.) Presumably all the details included in this group of autographs are faithfully reproduced in the Simrock editions used by Mandyczewski and Gál. Regrettably, the editors did not include as much documentary and critical apparatus as would be expected in a scholarly edition, so it is usually not possible to compare their work with the original editions, other than by laborious comparative analysis, detail by detail. Nor did they include sufficient specific information in their Editorial Reports (*Revisionsberichte*), and although Mandyczewski's annotations are more copious than Gál's, the reader is generally left unable to know whether, where, or when the *Sämtliche Werke* editions are more correct and reliable than the original editions.[28] Therefore, if the serious musician today is disinclined to accept an undocumented edition on faith alone, he might be advised to undertake the comparison of particular works with the original editions (for which the *SBV II* is indispensable) in order to verify his authentic text.

Plan, Function, and Use of the Catalog

Probably the most serious deficiency of the *Simrock Brahms Verzeichniss* is the lack of an introductory statement to describe the plan, function, and use of the catalog. It may be that this important element was one of the things excised by Brahms himself as superfluous, or it may be that the user at the turn of the century was familiar with the use of such an enumeration. Whatever the reasons for the omission, the full usefulness of the catalog cannot be realized until one knows what is contained within, what is not, and how the material is organized and

---

[28]A comprehensive critical analysis of the authenticity and editorial procedure of the *Sämtliche Werke* is an important aspect of the present author's research (see footnote 18).

treated. Much of this needed information must be supplied by deduction and extrapolation. The present section will supply many of the guides and clarifications needed for modern reference use. Some important corrections and additions will be found in the Supplements.

* * * * * * * * * * * * * * *

As stated on the *Inhalt* (Contents) leaf, the contents of the catalog are organized in a plan of two parts with an appendix, in the following outline (translated):[29]

I. Thematic Catalog, including a statement of all adaptations, publishers, and prices.
   A. Works with Opus Number (Opp. 1–121)
   B. Works without Opus Number

II. Catalogs and Index.
   1. Systematic Catalog, classified according to the media of performance
   2. Alphabetical Index of the titles and first lines of the collected vocal works

   Appendix.
      a) (Systematic) Summary of the Arrangements and Transcriptions
      b) Name and Subject Index

Each item in Part I consists of a complete entry of the composition(s) by identifying heading, original edition, thematic incipits, and specifications of settings, performing materials, and arrangements. The function of this scheme can be illustrated by a typical main entry:

It must be emphasized that the works cataloged are the original standard versions as well as arrangements by Brahms published during his lifetime, and by which he evidently wished to be remembered and perpetuated. The numerous arrangements and transcriptions, including orchestrations, he had made of other com-

---

[29]With the exception of *SBV I*, which consists of Works with Opus Number only through Op. 101, and subdivides the Works without Opus Number into separate classes for voice, organ, and pianoforte, this outline obtains for each issue of the catalog.

posers' works, though most of them were published during his lifetime, are excluded from this catalog.

An additional major work, the *Elf Choralvorspiele für die Orgel*, was issued posthumously—erroneously as the "sole posthumous work" (*Einziges nachgelassenes Werk*)—around 1902, as Opus 122. It may be regretted that it was given a number, for it is more appropriately classified with the Works without Opus Number.[30] The other works which were discovered and published posthumously in the course of the subsequent two decades by the Deutsche Brahms-Gesellschaft and Breitkopf & Härtel (*Sämtliche Werke*), as well as by several other publishers, are compositions and arrangements which Brahms had rejected and withheld from publication. It is clear, therefore, that Fritz Simrock, unlike his successors, respected the composer's wishes in confining the present catalog to the collected works in original editions and authorized arrangements published during the lifetime of Brahms.

[Part I. Thematic Catalog: Main Entries]

IDENTIFYING HEADING—The Works with Opus Number do not necessarily correspond to the actual chronology of the works, either to exact order of composition or of publication. Much interchanging was obviously if not admittedly practiced. The sets of songs, especially, were frequently assembled partly from new and partly from existing works to form a collective *opus*. The Works without Opus Number were presumably left unnumbered because of their character as arrangements of other composers' pieces, as compositional studies, or as anonymous publications. The bulk of these are early works.

The *titles* include both proper and generic titles, classification by performance medium, often the key, and where appropriate the authors and sources of texts, and dedicatory statements. In most instances, the heading material is original with Brahms and expressly preferred by him. Here, the notable exceptions are English captions, titles, and identity of translators—for Brahms would not accept any responsibility for translations of his German songs.

The *dedications* offer a fascinating study in themselves, for it will be noticed that Brahms did not publicly inscribe more than thirty-five works, and one of them (Opus 49/4) was only quietly inscribed at that. He was spasmodic in dedicating his works until about 1882, after which he virtually ceased the practice. Many

---

[30]It might be conjectured that the alleged composition date (1896) of the chorale preludes could suggest that *SBV II* was prepared in 1896, i.e., before Brahms' death and before the new works could be published, but the actual reasons for the omission of Op. 122 are more likely related to the fact that the composer made revisions in the engraver's layout immediately before his death. After death, his complicated estate was in litigation, and it was not until 1902 that Op. 122 could be issued; it was first cataloged in *SBV IV* (1903).

other works were unquestionably dedicated to members of a most select group of very close personal friends, as we surmise from examining the autographs, but the printed editions do not reveal this fact. In all his dedications he was evidently very reticent and selective in granting such favors only to the most admired of his sincere friends and benefactors, irrespective of their worldly influence, and obviously without consideration of possible benefit to the sales promotion of his editions. A highly interesting fact that can be gleaned from Kalbeck is that Brahms sometimes composed a work under inspiration or to the memory of one friend while publicly dedicating it to another.[31] That he apparently made a deliberate distinction between the two nearly synonymous past-participles, *gewidmet and zugeeignet*, in the printed dedications, can lead to the interesting hypothesis that the former verb, more customarily used by other authors, was reserved to distinguish a more personal and affectionate, less formal relationship; while the latter verb was used more often, and evidently for more complimentary, honorific, and formal dedications. If an apparent contradiction suggests itself in the treatment of several of his most intimate friends (such as Joachim, Clara Schumann, Gänsbacher, Hanslick, Billroth, Engelmann, and Allgeyer), the explanation can be discovered in (a) the public and professional stature of the recipient in comparison to that of the composer at the time of dedication, or (b) the fact that a close friendship had not yet developed.

Brahms dedicated compositions to the following persons:

Widmung:
Bettina von Arnim (Op. 3)
Albert Dietrich (Op. 7)
Julius Otto Grimm (Op. 10)
Julie Schumann (Op. 23)
Amalie Joachim (Op. 28)
Julius Stockhausen (Op. 33)
Anna von Hessen (Op. 34)
Philipp Spitta (Op. 74)
Elisabet von Herzogenberg (Op. 79)
Hans von Bülow (Op. 108)
Wiener Singacademie (WoO *Deutsche Volkslieder*)
Robert and Clara Schumann children (WoO *Volkskinderlieder*)

Zueignung:
Joseph Joachim (Opp. 1, 77)
Clara Schumann (Opp. 2, 9, WoO *Gavotte*)
Ernst Ferdinand Wenzel (Op. 4)
Ida von Hohenthal (Op. 5)
Luise and Minna Japha (Op. 6)
Reinhard von Dalwigk (Op. 25)
Elisabeth Rösing (Op. 26)
Anna von Hessen (Op. 34*bis*)
Josef Gänsbacher (Op. 38)
Eduard Hanslick (Op. 39)
Theodor Billroth (Op. 51)
Kaiser Wilhelm I. (Op. 55)
Theodor Wilhelm Engelmann (Op. 67)
Julius Allgeyer (Op. 75)
Henriette Feuerbach (Op. 82)
Eduard Marxsen (Op. 83)
Georg von Sachsen-Meiningen (Op. 89)
Carl Petersen (Op. 109)
Max Klinger (Op. 121)

---

[31]Throughout Kalbeck, op. cit., in reference to circumstances surrounding the composition of various works.

ORIGINAL EDITION—In the data concerning the original edition (*Original-Ausgabe*) are the *imprint* of the place, publisher, and year of publication, and the *collation* indicating the publisher's number (usually identical with plate number), format of the score (*Partitur*) and sometimes of the parts (*Stimmen*), pagination (*Paginierung*) of the music, exclusive of title page and other preliminary matter, and price.

Some words of caution are important. All these descriptive facts apply to the so-called "original edition," but because of the ambiguous meaning of that loosely defined term one cannot be certain without further analysis that the original edition is necessarily the same as the *first edition* (*erste Ausgabe*). In most instances it is, but the imprint and collation should not be used for confirmation because the same data may be applicable to numerous later impressions—or even editions—beyond the first issue. The difficulty emanates from the meaning and use of *Original-Ausgabe*, for it is apparent that Simrock and Rieter-Biedermann, and probably the others as well, used the term to distinguish between what were in fact the composer's standard versions/editions and the subsequent variant versions, even if made or authorized by the composer, such as the "transposed editions" (*Transponirten Ausgaben*), arrangements and transcriptions (*Arrangements, Bearbeitungen*), and other adaptations or revisions. (These distinctions are elaborated upon under *Specifications, Materials, Arrangements,* below.) The meaning of *Original-Ausgabe* also extends to signify the editions, of whatever generation, issued by the original publisher.

In the handling of *publication dates* none of the publishers was entirely scrupulous: very often an original-edition date will be a year or more earlier or later than actual publication, depending upon which part of the year the edition was issued. Such errors appear on the music and are repeated in the catalog. Breitkopf & Härtel and Rieter-Biedermann were somewhat more meticulous and C. F. Spina and Bartholf Senff, much more meticulous. But Simrock, starting with Opus 59, became progressively more unreliable, as Kalbeck confirms.[32]

The *prices* quoted in *SBV II* are especially undependable, for they refer to the current issue (the one available in 1897) which naturally might be priced higher than the first issue of the original edition, and lower than later issues. Simrock rarely printed the price on the title pages, so it is not possible to depend on a statement of a Simrock price in the catalog to confirm an identification of a particular impression of sheet music. Rieter-Biedermann, on the contrary, usually printed the prices, but they were rarely changed during the history of the firm. When Rieter's editions were later reissued in C. F. Peters' jackets, the prices were often changed, although the physical features were not.

---

[32]Kalbeck, op. cit., I/2, 465.

The imprint and collation data, therefore, are reliable within these limits, and are most valuable in determining whether or not a particular print is a composer's standard version/edition. They are not helpful, however, in identifying particular issues of an original edition. For this function, other criteria, mostly internal, must be considered: alterations in title pages and degrees of fuzziness in typography— caused by excessive reprintings from old plates or from cheaper lithographic transfers (*Umdrücke*) from plates to an offset medium — and progressively cheaper and more brittle papers are the principal evidences of later issues.[33] An interesting observation, not noted in the catalog, is the striking similarity in physical appearance between the Brahms editions issued by different publishers. This is due no doubt to the fact that one engraver-printer (Carl Gottlieb Röder in Leipzig) did the work for Rieter-Biedermann, Simrock, Peters, and probably others. Breitkopf & Härtel did their own engraving and printing, so their editions are distinctively different in appearance.

THEMATIC INCIPITS—The thematic incipits are given in actual or condensed piano score for instrumental works, and in one or more additional staves for vocal works. Incipits of chamber and orchestral pieces are in piano reductions (*Klavierauszüge*), while vocal pieces and piano pieces are taken exactly from the original setting. In the incipits are essential elements of initial phrases usually of each principal section of the composition, together with tempo indications and words of expression, text sources and first lines of texts, dynamics, and vocal and instrumental cues. Only five works (Opp. 8, 45, 82, 83, 87) have metronome marks. Total numbers of measures (*Takte*) are included for instrumental introductions and selected internal sections. For solo vocal works the range (*Umfang*) of the voice is given, as well as English translations where applicable. In one instance (Opus 72/5) the source of the thematic motive is traced to the original composer (D. Scarlatti). The incipits seem to be very accurate. Only a scant five typographical errors were detected by Mandyczewski,[34] none of which was corrected in later issues of *SBV*.

SPECIFICATIONS, MATERIALS, ARRANGEMENTS—In this supplementary statement are listed all current (1897) editions, issues, arrangements, and transcriptions in basic specifications for the performing musician. The absence of most bibliographic information relating to imprint generally is to be interpreted as meaning that each item belongs to the publisher of the original edition, except when specifically noted otherwise. Collation data are also generally incomplete, but names of arrangers, prices, and, often, publication dates are given. Limitations notwithstanding, enough information is given for reasonably accurate identification of authentic variant versions prepared by Brahms himself (*vom Componisten*),

---

[33]See Deutsch for a highly detailed exposition of these complicated problems of bibliographic analysis for original editions and subsequent issues.

[34]Mandyczewski's marginal notes in his exemplar of *SBV I/II* (see page xvi, above). These errors are noted above in Supplement A: Addenda and Corrigenda to *SBV II*.

or prepared by others and recognized by him. The list is especially important for confirming which versions in the flood-wake of posthumous variant versions are authentic.

Generally, the order of items listed begins with supplementary specifications for the original edition, as instrumentation and voices of the full score. Then follow performing materials, as separate parts and extra parts (*Stimmen*), single issues (*Einzeln*), vocal scores, etc. Arranged and other variant editions are next. These include transposed editions (*Transponirten Ausgabe*), separate issues (*Einzel-Ausgabe*), easy editions (*Leichte Ausgabe*), and arrangements (*Arrangements, arrangirt*), revisions (*Überarbeitungen*), and adaptations or transcriptions (*Übertragungen* and *Bearbeitungen*).

The distinction between the various types of *Arrangements* and *Bearbeitungen* is by no means clear, although a pattern—inconsistent at best—seems to imply that arrangements constitute an adaptation within the species context for limited performance and study purposes (e.g., Concerto for Violin, Cello, and Orchestra, Opus 102, arranged for Violin, Cello, and Piano). Transcriptions are more or less extreme changes of medium for public performance and involve some degree of recomposition by the arranger to make idiomatic adjustments (e.g., Opus 102 transcribed for piano, four-hands).[35] Precisely what alterations were made in revised issues or editions and in the sometimes several versions of piano arrangements of a given work can be determined only by patient comparative textual analysis of individual cases. In subsequent issues of *SBV*, notices of other materials and arrangements, in the several classes, were added by inserted lines of type, while some of the existing items were deleted without notice.

The question of Brahms' own relationship to the numerous arrangements, transcriptions, and translations is a complex and highly interesting inquiry in its own right. It may be said that he viewed the whole situation with very mixed emotions, most of them not very pleasant. He saw no reason to publish piano arrangements of chamber or orchestral scores, for he considered the transfer of one idiom to another medium a distortion of the standard version, and he felt that the amateur pianist should be able to read from open score and reduce at sight, as he himself did. But although he evidently held to this belief throughout his

---

[35]It is perhaps worthy of note that in the English-language catalog issued by Simrock, through their agent Lengnick (Schott & Co.), London, 1906, the exclusive term for all such adaptations is "arrangements." If Simrock, in the German catalog, insisted on using both the French *arrangement* and the German *Bearbeitung*, both separately and apparently interchangeably, our only hope for ultimate clarification is to accept "arangement" as the generic classification, in which the other terms are virtually synonymous. One can commiserate with the remarkable scholar, editor, and friend of Brahms and Simrock, Mandyczewski, who evidently gave up in exasperation as he failed to understand a similar situation and wrote in the margin of his *SBV*, "Das ist nicht ganz klar, [signed] Mandy."

career, he cooperated, albeit reluctantly, with his publishers by preparing his own reductions and arrangements—but not transcriptions—for publication, realizing that thereby more people would have opportunity to play and know his music. In all, he prepared for publication some forty works in two- and four-hand reductions and arrangements for one and two pianos. Some of them, particularly for four hands/two pianos, clearly were made simultaneously with, if not before, the standard versions, as a stage in his creative process. All the while, he complained to Fritz Simrock that these variant versions, especially the transcriptions, too often appeared before the standard versions had had time to become known.

For transcriptions he had no patience whatever, unless he made them himself as separate compositions (such as the *Variations on a Theme of Haydn*, Op. 56b), which he refused to consider as variants of standard versions.[36] His contempt was intense for Fritz Simrock's rampant commercialism in having a popular work transcribed for every conceivable medium and taste, in order to assure maximum sales. The ubiquitous *Wiegenlied*, Op. 49/4, for instance, became a particularly sore point with Brahms because Simrock had it adapted for piano solo; paraphrased for two hands, four hands, and six hands (!); embellished as *fantasies* (twice); improvised upon; arranged for piano and violin, piano and flute, piano, flute, and violin (or piano and two flutes); and transcribed for four-part *Männerchor*. This exploitation evoked Brahms' most wrathful sarcasm and impelled him to ask Simrock if they should not also bring out a version in minor for naughty and sicky children.[37] With the additional versions brought out after the passing of both Brahms and Fritz— another paraphrase, another *fantasie*, and arrangements for piano and cello, for harp, for zither, for mixed chorus, and for harmonium and piano, among others—it is possible that the sickly and the maladjusted were well consoled, indeed.

Brahms clearly had very little esteem for the musical competence and taste of Robert Keller, whom he evidently considered pedestrian and dubbed a Philistine.[38] But he had a compassionate regard for his need to earn a livelihood, so he kept his estimation from Simrock.[39] Keller's arrangements for piano began around 1873 when he was apparently engaged by Simrock. During 1878 he seems to have hired out to Melchior Rieter-Biedermann's son-in-law and successor, Edmund Astor, to prepare two arrangements of Brahms, after which he moved back to Simrock to amass a total of some sixty adaptations during the ensuing decade. The progression of arrangers is confusing because of the transiency be-

---

[36]See the author's forthcoming edition, *Brahms, Variations on a Theme of Haydn* (A Norton Critical Score), New York: W. W. Norton, ca. 1974, for an extended discussion of Brahms' arrangements and transcriptions.

[37]Stephenson, op. cit., 18.

[38]Stephenson, ibid., 17.

[39]Kalbeck, op. cit., IV/1, 90.

tween the various publishers by some of the same individuals, some of whom were obviously recommended by Brahms to do arranging and transcribing, while many others could not possibly have had his blessing. One cannot imagine Brahms having much enthusiasm for the work of Salomon Jadassohn, Ludwig Stark, or Edwin H. Lemare, for example, to take only a few names from the large list of formidable musicians whose aesthetics were rather far from his own, but he undoubtedly felt kindly toward his friends, particularly Theodor Kirchner, Friedrich Hermann, J. Carl Eschmann, Richard Heuberger, and Dvořák.

The largest arranging and transcribing assignments were done by Keller, Hermann, Kirchner, and Paul Klengel. Hermann, who specialized in piano and strings and/or winds, started with Breitkopf & Härtel, moved to Rieter, and culminated with Simrock. He was a product of the Leipzig Conservatory and remained there as an outstanding violin teacher and member of the Gewandhaus Orchestra. Kirchner, a bit younger than Hermann, was the first student at Mendelssohn's Conservatory. His subsequent career as organist, teacher, and composer was strongly influenced by Mendelssohn and Schumann, and, lastly, by Brahms who considered him a worthy composer and arranger, and a good friend. He held important posts in Winterthur, Zürich, Meiningen, Würzburg, Leipzig, Dresden, and Hamburg. Klengel, much younger, also studied at the Conservatory and at the University of Leipzig (*D.Phil.*), then directed various important choral groups in Leipzig, Stuttgart, and New York (German Liederkranz Society, 1898–1902). He finally returned to the Leipzig Conservatory as teacher and conductor. It is certainly notable that the Leipzig tradition of neo-classic Romanticism was abundantly associated with the propagation of Brahms through these men and some of the other arrangers and publishers. True it was indeed, with respect to Brahms, that the heart of music was in Vienna, while the head was in Leipzig.

[*Part II. Catalogs and Index*]

The systematic catalog in Part II is classified according to the media of performance, divided first by instrumental music and second by vocal music. Only the standard versions are included in the list, as well as in the following alphabetical index of the titles and first lines of the collected vocal works. But again the observation should be made that these listings are complete only through 1897.

[*Appendix*]

In the Appendix to the *SBV*, the systematic summary of the arrangements and transcriptions is also classified by media of performance, and presumably includes all of the variant versions made by Brahms and by the numerous arrangers for the original publishers. While some of the chosen media appear rather exotic for arrangements of Brahms' conceptions, the variety and proportion of sonorous possibilities increased after 1897 to permit the widest imaginable combinations, including "Parisian orchestra,"[40] string orchestra, and military orchestra, in nearly all manner of options. Perhaps the most surprising concession to the new times was the publication of the *Requiem* in a "tonic sol-fa" notated edition for British consumption. Certainly, by 1910, and the last issue of the *Simrock Brahms Verzeichniss*, with the advent of arrangers and transcribers such as Wilhelm Altmann, Healey Willan, Paul Juon, and Max Reger, the world had come to know Brahms in a somewhat different context and dimension.

---

[40]A "Parisian orchestra," according to Simrock's English-language catalog is comprised of violin, violoncello, flute, trumpet, pianoforte (harmonium ad libitum). See also footnote 35.

SUPPLEMENT A

Addenda and Corrigenda to *SBV II*

A conscientious effort has been made to verify most of the data printed in the identifying heading, imprint and collation, and thematic incipits of each entry. No thorough attempt has been made, however, to verify the data comprising the specifications, materials, and arrangements listed below the incipits. For to do so would require an exhaustive search for copies of all issues for documentation, and far more detailed analysis of the various versions than evidently has been undertaken by any bibliographer. This important task will have to be deferred to the future.

It will be observed that most of the data for which additions and corrections are offered here pertain to publication dates of the original editions. Undeniably, many if not all of these inaccuracies were intentionally perpetrated by the publisher of the catalog and often by the publishers of the music, presumably for commercial reasons. (See the brief discussion of this problem on page xxvii of the Introduction.) The other elements in the entries are remarkably accurate.

The addenda and corrigenda that follow have been derived from standard and specialized sources of Brahmsiana, particularly catalogs, bibliographies, and miscellaneous bibliographic notes. Each issue of the *SBV* has been collated and compared, and some of the same and other catalogs and indexes have been scanned for marginal corrections written by European bibliographic scholars. The principal documentation has been extracted from the following items; the surname of the authority is added parenthetically after the emendation:

Brahms, Johannes. Autograph Catalog *(Notizkalendar)*, unpublished, Wiener Stadtbibliothek, J. Nr. 32886 N.

Deutsch, Otto Erich. "The First Editions of Brahms," *The Music Review* I/2–3 (May & August 1940), 123–43, 255–78.

Gál, Hans. *Revisionsberichte* of *Johannes Brahms Sämtliche Werke*, Bde. I–X.

Kalbeck, Max. *Johannes Brahms*, 4 vols. in 8.

Mandyczewski, Eusebius. *Revisionsberichte* of *Johannes Brahms Sämtliche Werke*, Bde. XI–XXVI, and/or marginal notes in the Gesellschaft der Musikfreunde exemplar of *SBV I/II*.

Orel, Alfred. "Ein eigenhändiges Werkverzeichnis von Brahms," *Die Musik* XXIX/8 (May 1937), 529–41. [A transcription and analysis of Brahms' autograph catalog.]

The data published by Alfred von Ehrmann in his Brahms *Verzeichnis* have been considered but not included here.

PAGE	OPUS	ADDENDA AND CORRIGENDA
Page 1.	Opus 2	*Publication date:* February 1854 (Brahms, Deutsch), 1853 (Mandyczewski).
Page 2.	Opus 3	*Publication date:* December 1853 (Brahms, Deutsch).
Page 7.	Opus 8	*Publication date:* November 1854 (Brahms, Kalbeck, Gál, Deutsch).
Page 8.	Opus 11	*Publication date:* December 1860 (Brahms), January 1861 (Deutsch).
Page 9.	Opus 12	*Publication date:* December 1860 (Brahms), January 1861 (Deutsch). *Arrangements:* The "Clavierauszug mit Gesang" arranged by Brahms (Cf. *SBV II*, 173).

Page 9. Opus 13   *Publication date:* December 1860 (Brahms), January 1861 (Mandyczewski, Deutsch).
Arrangements: The "Clavierauszug mit Gesang" arranged by Brahms (Cf. *SBV II*, 173).

Page 9. Opus 14   *Publication date:* December 1860 (Brahms), January 1861 (Deutsch).

Page 10. Opus 15   *Publication date:* December 1860 (Brahms), 1861/2 (Deutsch).
Plate number: 170 (No. 815 is the octavo score of 1875).

Page 11. Opus 16   *Publication date:* Winter 1860 (Brahms), November 1860 (Deutsch). The second edition, revised by Brahms, was dated 1875, but printed November 1876 (Deutsch).

Page 12. Opus 17   *Alternative medium:* The "Pianobegleitung" is by Brahms (Cf. *SBV II*, 173).
Publication date: November 1860 (Brahms), February 1861 (Deutsch).

Page 12. Opus 18   *Publication date:* January 1862 (Brahms), December 1861 (Deutsch).

Page 14. Opus 20   *Publication date:* March 1862 (Brahms).

Page 15. Opus 21/1   *Publication date:* March 1862 (Brahms, Deutsch), 1861 (Mandyczewski).

Page 15. Opus 21/2   *Publication date:* March 1862 (Brahms, Deutsch), 1861 (Mandyczewski).

Page 16. Opus 23   *Publication date:* Beginning of 1863 (Brahms, Mandyczewski), January 1863 (Deutsch).

Page 18. Opus 27   *Title: recte "Der 13. Psalm."* Brahms' autograph catalog gives the correct number for the Psalm, but the error was not corrected in *SBV* until the third issue (1902).

Page 18. Opus 28   *Remarks:* Opp. 27 & 28 are reversed in Brahms' autograph catalog; thus the Psalm was originally Op. 28 and the duets Op. 27. But he indicated that the Psalm was published before the duets.

Page 19. Opus 29   *Arrangements:* The "Klavierauszuge" are by Brahms (Cf. *SBV II*, 173).

Page 21. Opus 32   *Publication date:* 1864 (Deutsch), Winter 1865 (Brahms).

Page 23. Opus 33   *Publication dates:* Complete opus issued in two parts: Hefte I, II, Spring 1865; Hefte III–V, 1869, not 1868 (Kalbeck, Deutsch).

Page 27. Opus 34   *Publication date:* 1866 (Brahms), December 7, 1865 (Deutsch).

Page 27. Opus 34bis   *Publication date:* September 1871 (Brahms), 1872 (Deutsch).

Page 29. Opus 37   *Publication date:* 1865 (Brahms), 1866 (Deutsch).

Page 30. Opus 39   *Publication date:* 1866 (Brahms), September 1866 (Deutsch).

Page 31. Opus 40   *Publication date:* November 1866 (Deutsch).

Page 32. Opus 42   *Remarks:* The "Clavierbegleitung" is by Brahms (Cf. *SBV II*, 173).

Page 36. Opus 45   *Publication date:* 1868/9 (Deutsch), 1868 (Mandyczewski).

Page 46. Opus 50   *Incipits:* Last incipit *(Allegro non troppo)*, add bass clef to signature in voice staff (Mandyczewski).
Arrangements: The "Clavierauszug mit Text" is by Brahms (Cf. *SBV II*, 173).

Page 52. Opus 53   *Publication date:* October 1869 (Brahms).
Plate number: Number 7034 is the second edition, ca. 1871 (Deutsch).
Arrangements: The "Clavierauszug" is by Brahms (Cf. *SBV II*, 173).

Page 53. Opus 54   *Arrangements:* The "Clavierauszug" in both editions is by Brahms (Cf. *SBV II*, 173).

Page 54.   Opus 55   *Arrangements:* The "Clavierauszug" in both editions and the arrangement for "Pianoforte zu vier Händen" are by Brahms (Cf. *SBV II,* 172, 173).

Page 54.   Opus 56a   *Publication date:* Autumn 1873 (Brahms), January 1874 (Deutsch).

Page 55.   Opus 56b   *Publication date:* Autumn 1873 (Brahms), November "1873" (Deutsch).

Page 66.   Opus 64   *Plate Number:* Number 1461 is the second edition, ca. 1880 (Deutsch).

Page 74.   Opus 70   *Remarks:* "Abendregen" was first published by E. W. Fritzsch, 1875.

Page 82.   Opus 78   *Publication date:* September 1879 (Brahms), November 1879 (Deutsch).

Page 84.   Opus 82   *Arrangements:* The "Clavierauszug" is by Brahms (Cf. *SBV II,* 173).

Page 90.   Opus 87   *Publication date:* December 1882 (Deutsch).

Page 91.   Opus 88   *Publication date:* December 1882 (Deutsch).

Pages 91-92.   *Publication date:* February 1884 (Deutsch), 1883 (Mandyczewski).
      Opus 89   *Arrangements:* The "Clavierauszug" is by Brahms (Cf. *SBV II,* 173).

Page 92.   Opus 90   *Arrangements:* The principal two-piano arrangement is by Brahms, as is an unlisted one-piano (four-hand) version (Cf. *SBV II,* 172).

Page 96.   Opus 93b   *Publication date:* January? "1884" (Deutsch), 1885 (Mandyczewski).

Page 105.   Opus 102   *Arrangements:* The "Clavierbegleitung" is by Brahms (Cf. *SBV II,* 171).

Page 107.   Opus 103   *Incipits:* No. 7, measure 2, first note for voice should read D, not Eb (Mandyczewski).

Page 108.   Opus 104   *Publication date:* 1888 (Deutsch).

Page 109.   Opus 105   *Publication date:* 1888 (Deutsch).

Page 110.   Opus 106   *Publication date:* 1888 (Deutsch).

Page 111.   Opus 107   *Publication date:* 1888 (Deutsch).

Page 113.   Opus 109   *Incipits:* No. 1, measure 1, 2nd note in tenor should read C, not E (Mandyczewski).

Page 115.   Opus 112   *Publication date:* 1892 (Deutsch).

Page 116.   Opus 113   *Publication date:* 1892 (Deutsch).

Page 120.   Opus 115   *Incipits:* Last incipit *(Un poco meno mosso),* measure 2, 3rd note in bass should read as eighth, not quarter (Mandyczewski).

Page 123.   Opus 118   *Incipits:* No. 6, measure 3, 2nd note in treble should read as eighth, not quarter (Mandyczewski).

Page 126.   Opus 121   *Arrangements:* "Ausgabe für Alt oder Baryton": In the second parenthetical sentence read *"eine Octave höher,"* not *"tiefer"* (Mandyczewski).

Page 127.   [WoO]   *Publication date:* 1894 (Deutsch).

Page 133.   Album   *Remarks:* Transcriptions of vocal works for violoncello and piano: Opp. 86/2, 105/1, 94/4, 49/4, 3/1, 71/5.

Page 141.   [WoO]   *Publication date:* 1st edition, G. H. Wigand, 1854. The imprint date in
      (Mond-   the entry actually refers to the 2nd edition, 1872.
      nacht)

Page 143.   [WoO]   *Remarks:* *"Ohne Namen des Autors"* signifies that the *Volkskinderlieder* was published without Brahms' name on the edition.

Page 146.   [WoO]   *Publication date:* 1882 (Deutsch).
      (Choral-
      vorspiel
      und Fuge)

Page 146. [WoO]   *Remarks:* Breitkopf & Härtel published the first edition as a *Beilage zu*
           (Fuge)   *AMZ* II/29, in 1864. It was reprinted separately by them in 1883. Simrock
                      published the second edition as a transfer (Pl. no. 9020) in 1888
                      (Deutsch).

Page 147. [WoO]   *Publication date:* Probably published in 1872 because it was composed
           (Gavotte) in that year.

Page 148. [WoO]   *Plate numbers:* The plate numbers for Hefte I, II given here are for
                      the third issue of the original edition. The first-edition numbers were
                      336 & 337 (Deutsch).

SUPPLEMENT B
Abbreviations for *SBV II*

à	= at (price)
arr.	arrangirt = arranged (by)
Bd.	Band = volume
bearb.	bearbeitet = arranged, transcribed
Br.	Bratsche = viola
C. Bass	Contra Bass = double bass
Cl., Clar.	Clarinette(n) = clarinet(s)
Contrafag.	Contrafagott(e) = contrabassoon(s)
Dcbr.	Dezember = December
deutsch.	deutschen(em) = German
engl.	englisch(en, em) = English
f.	für = for
Fag.	Fagott(e) = bassoon(s)
Fl.	Flöte(n) = flute(s)
geb.	geboren = born (née)
gem.	gemischten = mixed
Gr.	Grosses = great, grand, large
gr. 8°	grosse octavo = royal octavo (approx. $6\frac{3}{4}$ x $9\frac{1}{2}$ in.)
Hfte.	Hefte = books
Hob., Ob.	Hoboen, Oboen = oboes
instr.	Instrument (e) = instrument(s)
kl.	kleine = small
Königl.	Königliche = royal
M., Mk.	Mark (Reichsmark) = 100 Pfennige
m.	mit = with
m. v.	mezza voce
n.	netto = net (price)
od.	oder = or
Orig.-Ausg.	Original-Ausgabe = original edition
Pag.	Paginierung = pagination
Pauk.	Pauken = timpani
Pf., Pfge.	Pfennig(e) = .01 of a Mark
Pfte., Pianof.	Pianoforte
Pos.	Posaune(n) = trombone(s)
Pr.	Preis = price

Pr. compl.	Preis complet = price complete
Qu.	Quartett = strings (quartet)
4°	quarto = approx. 9 x 12 in.
S.	Seit = page
s.	siehe = see
S.A.T.B.	Sopran, Alt, Tenor, Bass
Singst.	Singstimmen = (vocal) voices, parts
Sopr.	Sopran = soprano
st.	stimmen, stimmig(en) = voices, parts
Tromp.	Trompete = trumpet
u.	und = and
übersetz.	übersetzung = adaptation, translation
unis.	unisono = unison
v.	von = by, of
Vcll., Vcell., Vc.	Violoncell = violoncello
vgl.	vergleiche(n, m) = compare (see)
Viol.	Violine(n) = violin(s)
vorm.	vormals = formerly
weibl.	weiblichen = female
z.	zu = to, for

SUPPLEMENT C

Bibliographic Description of *SBV I–VI*

The history of the *Simrock Brahms Verzeichniss* is complicated at best. Between 1887 and 1910, six issues were published, each of which contained unspecified alterations of previous content. Without a critical comparison of all six issues, it is by no means clear what these changes were. Furthermore, N. Simrock also issued a number of non-thematic, promotional sales catalogs as leaflets or pamphlets in 1897, 1903, 1906, and 1908, and perhaps others. These should not be confused with the *SBV*. (They are identified in the Bibliography on page xlix).

What follows is a bibliographic description of each issue of the *SBV*, summarizing the alterations found therein.

[*SBV I*]

THEMATISCHES / VERZEICHNISS / DER BISHER / IM DRUCK ERSCHIENENEN WERKE / VON / JOHANNES BRAHMS. / [wavy rule] / NEBST SYSTEMATISCHEM VER-ZEICHNISS / UND REGISTERN. / [ornamented rule] / N. SIMROCK IN BERLIN / 1887.

Pl. no. 8607. 3 preliminary leaves, 134 pages, ± 28.5 x 19 cm. (bound).
This edition contains *Werke mit Opuszahl* through Op. 101 and eight *Werke ohne Opuszahl* (*Mondnacht, Deutsche Volkslieder Hefte I–II, Volkskinderlieder, Choralvorspiel und Fuge, Fuge in As moll, Studien für das Pianoforte, Gavotte von C. W. Gluck, Ungarische Tänze*).

Library of Congress (*ex libris* Max Kalbeck) and Gesellschaft der Musikfreunde (*ex libris* Eusebius Mandyczewski), Vienna. These two exemplars are bound with the supplementary pages from the 1897 (second) issue and contain written-in emendations by the two Brahms scholars.

[*SBV II*]

THEMATISCHES / VERZEICHNISS / SÄMMTLICHER / IM DRUCK ERSCHIENENEN WERKE / VON / JOHANNES BRAHMS. / [wavy rule] / NEBST SYSTEMATISCHEM VER ZEICHNISS / UND REGISTERN. / [ornamented rule] / N. SIMROCK IN BERLIN / 1897.

Pl. no. 8607. 2 p.l., 175 p., ± 28.5 x 19 cm. (bound).
This second issue is an enlargement of the original edition to include the additional works composed and published through 1897. The title page was altered, and some important changes and additions incorporated within the original page-plates. Forty-one new plates were engraved to accommodate the additional compositions and the expanded catalogs and indexes. New pages 105–140 were inserted between original pages 104–105; pagination of original pages 105–134 changed to 141–175.

Library of Congress and Gesellschaft der Musikfreunde, as above.

[*SBV III*]

THEMATISCHES / VERZEICHNISS / SÄMMTLICHER / IM DRUCK ERSCHIENENEN WERKE / VON / JOHANNES BRAHMS. / [wavy rule] / NEBST SYSTEMATISCHEM VER- ZEICHNISS / UND REGISTERN. / [wavy rule] / NEUE AUSGABE. / [ornamented rule] / N. SIMROCK IN BERLIN / 1902.

Pl. no. 8607. 2 p.l., 175 p., ± 27.5 x 19 cm. (bound).
This extremely rare "new issue" is a reprint of the 1897 issue, with altered title page and numerous additions of arrangements made by other musicians incorporated within the entries by added lines of type. Alterations in the page-plates were made to change Breitkopf imprints in favor of Simrock, to substitute some later editions for originals, and to add some transposed editions for high and low voices. The prices quoted here are the same as in *SBV II*. Otherwise, it is almost as accurate as *SBV II*, but very misleading to the uninformed user.

Princeton University Library.

[*SBV IV*]

THEMATISCHES / VERZEICHNISS / SÄMMTLICHER / IM DRUCK ERSCHIENENEN WERKE / VON / JOHANNES BRAHMS. / [wavy rule] / NEBST SYSTEMATISCHEM VER- ZEICHNISS / UND REGISTERN. / [wavy rule] / NEUE AUSGABE. / [ornamented rule] / N. SIMROCK, G.M.B.H., BERLIN / 1903.

Pl. no. 8607. 2 p.l., 175 p., ± 28.5 x 19 cm. (bound).
The first issue of the reorganized Simrock firm *(Gesellschaft mit Beschränkter Haftung)*. Here further alterations have been made without any notice, although the arrangements and editions which differ from those in *SBV II* are apparently the same as those listed in 1902, but with altered prices. The most significant alteration is the addition of Op. 122, which was added as p. 127. To justify the pagination, pp. 127–151 were renumbered as pp. 128–152 by using one former blank leaf (counted as p. 152). More misleading than *SBV III*.

Library of Congress copy contains written-in additions and corrections in the autographs of O. G. Sonneck and another bibliographer.

[*SBV V*]

THEMATISCHES / VERZEICHNISS / SÄMMTLICHER / IM DRUCK ERSCHIENENEN WERKE / VON / JOHANNES BRAHMS. / [wavy rule] / NEBST SYSTEMATISCHEM VER-ZEICHNISS/ UND REGISTERN. / [wavy rule] / NEUE VERMEHRTE AUSGABE. / PREIS MK. 4.—NETTO. / [ornamented rule] / N. SIMROCK, G.M.B.H., BERLIN / 1904.

Pl. no. 8607. 2 p.l., 175 p., ± 28.5 x 19 cm. (bound).
An altered reprint of *SBV IV*, with the same types of alterations as before. Incorporated are newer arrangements by other musicians for harmonium, harp, etc., as well as miniature score editions (for the first time) ; some more original editions have been deleted. French texts appear for some vocal works. Some price changes appear without notice. A particularly misleading and unreliable catalog.

Newberry Library, Chicago.

[*SBV VI*]

THEMATISCHES / VERZEICHNISS / SÄMMTLICHER / IM DRUCK ERSCHIENENEN WERKE / VON / JOHANNES BRAHMS. / [wavy rule] / NEBST SYSTEMATISCHEM VER-ZEICHNISS / UND REGISTERN. / [wavy rule] / NEUE VERMEHRTE AUSGABE. / PREIS MK. 4.—NETTO. / [ornamented rule] / N. SIMROCK, G.M.B.H., BERLIN / 1910.

Pl. no. 8607. 2 p.l., 175 p., ± 28.5 x 19 cm. (bound).
Final issue, a varied reprint of the previous issue, not otherwise a "new enlarged issue," but still further removed from the authority of Brahms. Numerous new arrangers and transcribers appear with added editions of adaptations.

Smith College Library, Northampton, Mass. The National Union Catalog entry for this exemplar is not entirely correct.

Aided in part by the National Union Catalog of The Library of Congress, I have compiled below a list of locations for each issue of the *SBV*.

[*SBV I*]	Berkeley, University of California
	New Haven, Yale University
	Vienna, Gesellschaft der Musikfreunde
	Washington, D.C., Library of Congress
[*SBV II*]	Ann Arbor, University of Michigan
	Austin, University of Texas
	Baltimore, Peabody Institute
	Boston Public Library
	New York Public Library
	Poughkeepsie, Vassar College
	Vienna, Gesellschaft der Musikfreunde
	Washington, D.C., Library of Congress

[*SBV III*]   Cleveland Public Library
             Princeton, Princeton University

[*SBV IV*]   Washington, D.C., Library of Congress

[*SBV V*]   Chicago, Newberry Library

[*SBV VI*]   Berkeley, University of California
             Los Angeles, University of Southern California
             Northampton, Smith College

SUPPLEMENT D
Omitted Published Works

Listed in this supplement are the works omitted from the *Simrock Brahms Verzeichniss*. They are largely posthumous publications of minor compositions by Brahms, and some original and posthumous publications of his arrangements and editions of works of other composers. Only one of his works (Opus 122) received a posthumous Opus Number and was added to later issues of the catalog, beginning in 1903.

The works are identified and described briefly here by title, classification, and imprint of the original or first edition. Their places in the *Johannes Brahms Sämtliche Werke*, where applicable, are indicated by volume number and page. No collation data have been included because it has not been possible to examine many of the editions.

For a more comprehensive bibliographic description of the majority of the works, the reader is referred to Otto Erich Deutsch's bibliography, "The First Editions of Brahms," *(The Music Review*, I/3, 266–73), a principal source and authority for much of the present index. It must be cautioned, however, that sections C–J of Deutsch's bibliography are by no means free of error. Thematic incipits for all but a few of Brahms' posthumous Works without Opus Number (i.e., excluding arrangements and editions of other composers' works) are printed in Ehrmann's *Johannes Brahms, Thematisches Verzeichnis seiner Werke* (pp. 150–63). These several indexes have been collated with the standard sources for Brahms' work, including the *Sämtliche Werke*, and with various catalogs and indexes of manuscript collections in Europe and the United States. The card catalog and printed music collection of The Library of Congress have been invaluable.

As far as current knowledge extends, then, the present list contains most of the *published* musical work of Brahms. It does not, however, account for every one of his still unpublished efforts (and some posthumously published variants), and notably some arrangements, editions, and copies of works of numerous composers from the Renaissance through his own time. They remain in autographs in the Gesellschaft der Musikfreunde (Vienna) and in copyists' manuscripts in the Smith College Library (Northampton, Mass.), if not elsewhere as well.

An especially interesting class of Works without Opus Number is that consisting of arrangements of German folk-songs, songs, and canons made by Brahms during his years with the Hamburg *Frauenchor* (1859–1861). Some 126 pieces, in settings for women's voices, are extant in manuscripts prepared by members of the *Frauenchor*, presumably from Brahms' own scores (mostly no longer extant) and under his watchful eye. These Mss are now in the Drinker Collection at Smith College. Although absolute authentication of all these pieces as genuine Brahms arrangements or compositions is not yet possible (because they exist only in imperfect copies), enough evidence is available to support the conclusion that they are largely early essays—premature versions or prototypes, as it were—for later standard versions which he subsequently prepared for publication. Undoubtedly, Brahms regarded most of the early versions as unworthy of his imprimatur and intended them for destruction. (The presumably complete list of the total collection is found in Sophie Drinker's *Brahms and his Women's Choruses* [Merion, Pa.: The Author, 1952], appendix A. An incomplete general index, with collation, is included in *Folk Songs for Women's Voices Arranged by Johannes Brahms,* edited by Vernon Gotwals and Philip Keppler, *Smith College Music Archives* XV [Northampton, Mass.: Smith College, 1968], 53–8.)

Among the cache of pieces are some twenty-five unpublished arrangements of works of other composers and, most important, eighteen unknown folk-song arrangements and canons. The latter items remained unpublished until they appeared in editions by Henry S. Drinker (ca. 1940), Siegfried Kross (1964, 1965), and Gotwals and Keppler (1968). Siegmund Helms included several of the works first edited by Drinker, in his dissertation, *Die Melodiebildung in den Liedern von Johannes Brahms und ihr Verhältnis zu Volksliedern und volkstümlichen Weisen* [Berlin, 1967; printed Bamberg, 1968], and subsequently reprinted twenty-three of the Gotwals-Keppler editions as *Volksliedbearbeitungen für Frauenchor* in the series *Das 19. Jahrhundert* [Kassel: Bärenreiter, 1970]. In the present list, only the first editions of the arrangements for women's voices are given within the series or book title. The many arrangements which were subsequently rearranged by Brahms and published (thus, included in the *Sämtliche Werke*) are omitted here.

I. *Posthumous Work with Opus Number*

Opus 122. Elf Choralvorspiele für die Orgel. (Einziges nachgelassnes Werk.)
    Componirt in Ischl im Mai und Juni 1896. [Edited by E. Mandyczewski.] Zwei Hefte.
    Berlin: N. Simrock, 1902.
    Republished in *Sämtliche Werke* XVI, 28.
    (Reproduced on following page)

II. *Original and Posthumous Works without Opus Number*

(In chronological order of publication)

"Töne, lindernder Klang" (Canon für Sopran, Alt, Tenor und Bass).
    Leipzig: E. W. Fritzsch, 1872 (Lithographed facsimile in *Musikalisches Wochenblatt* III/4 [Jan. 19, 1872], 57).
    Republished in *Sämtliche Werke* XXI, 156.

"Mir lächelt kein Frühling" (Canon für Frauenstimmen).
    Leipzig: E. W. Fritzsch, 1881 (Printed in *Musikalisches Wochenblatt* XII/18 [April 28, 1881], 216).
    Republished in *Sämtliche Werke* XXI, 189.

"Wann? wann?" (L. Uhland), Canon für Sopran und Alt.
    Stuttgart: W. Spemann, 1885 (Lithographed facsimile in Emil Naumann's *Illustrierte Musikgeschichte* II, 1089).
    Republished in *Sämtliche Werke* XXI, 192.

Sonatensatz (Scherzo) für Violine und Pianoforte. Joseph Joachim gewidmet.
    Berlin: Deutsche Brahms-Gesellschaft, 1906 (*Publikationen,* No. 1).
    Republished in *Sämtliche Werke* X, 88.

Op. 122.
Elf Choralvorspiele für die Orgel.
(Einziges nachgelassenes Werk.)
Componirt in Ischl im Mai und Juni 1896.
ZWEI HEFTE.
N. Simrock G.m.b.H. in Berlin. 1902.
Heft I. Verlags-No 11726. [Pag. 3-19] Pr. 3 M. netto.
Heft II. Verlags-No 11727. [Pag. 2-13] Pr. 3 M. netto.

HEFT I.

No 1. Mein Jesu, der du mich.
My Jesus, thou who didst.

No 2. Herzliebster Jesu.
Saviour of my heart.
Adagio.

No 3. O Welt, ich muss dich lassen.
O world, I e'en must leave thee.

No 4. Herzlich thut mich erfreuen.
My inmost heart rejoiceth.

HEFT II.

No 5. Schmücke dich, o liebe Seele.
Decks thyself out, o my soul.

No 6. O wie selig seid ihr doch, ihr Frommen.
O how blessed, faithful spirits, are ye.
Molto moderato.

No 7. O Gott, du frommer Gott.
O God, thou Holiest.

No 8. Es ist ein' Ros' entsprungen.
A rose breaks into bloom.

No 9. Herzlich thut mich verlangen.
My inmost heart doth yearn.

No 10. Herzlich thut mich verlangen.
My inmost heart doth yearn.

No 11. O Welt, ich muss dich lassen.
O world, I e'en must leave thee.

Ausgabe für Pianoforte zu vier Händen von E. MANDYCZEWSKI. Heft I (1-5); Heft II (6-11) Pr. à 4 M.
„ „ „ „ zwei „ von PAUL JUON. Heft I (1-5); Heft II (6-11) Pr. à 4 M.
„ „ Harmonium von AUG. REINHARD. Heft I (1-5); Heft II (6-11) Pr. à 4 M.
Sechs Choralvorspiele. (No 4, 5, 8, 9, 10, 11.) für Pianoforte zu zwei Händen ausgewählt und übertragen von FERRUCIO BUSONI. Pr. 4 M.
Sechs Choralvorspiele. Ausgabe für Harmonium und Pianoforte von AUGUST REINHARD.
No 1. (Orig. Ausg. No 1). Mein Jesu, der du mich. Pr. 2.- M. No 4. (Orig. Ausg. No 8) Es ist ein' Ros' entsprungen. Pr. 1.50 M.
No 2. (Orig. Ausg. No 3). O Welt ich muss dich lassen. Pr. 1.50 M. No 5. (Orig. Ausg. No 9). Herzlich thut mich verlangen. Pr. 1.50 M.
No 3. (Orig. Ausg. No 4). Herzlich thut mich erfreuen. Pr. 1.50 M. No 6. (Orig. Ausg. No 11). O Welt ich muss dich lassen. Pr. 1.50 M.

8607

Reproduced in facsimile from *SBV IV.*

Zwei Cadenzen zu L. van Beethoven's Klavierkonzert in G dur, op. 58. [Edited by E. Mandyczewski.]
>
> Berlin: Deutsche Brahms-Gesellschaft, 1907 (*Publikationen*, No. 5).
> Republished in *Sämtliche Werke* XV, 112.

"O wie sanft" (Daumer), Kanon für vier Frauenstimmen.
>
> Berlin: Deutsche Brahms-Gesellschaft, 1908 (Printed in Max Kalbeck's *Johannes Brahms*
> II/1, 275–8).
> Republished in *Sämtliche Werke* XXI, 191.

Regenlied, Gedichte von Klaus Groth. Für eine Singstimme mit Begleitung des Pianoforte.
[Edited by Hermann Stange.]
>
> Berlin: Deutsche Brahms-Gesellschaft, 1908 (*Publikationen*, No. 6).
> Republished in *Sämtliche Werke* XXVI, 64.

Zwei Sarabanden für das Pianoforte. Nachgelassenes Werk. Mit einem Vorwort von Max Friedlaender und der Wiedergabe der Urschrift.
>
> Berlin: Deutsche Brahms-Gesellschaft, 1917 (*Publikationen*, No. 8).
> Republished in *Sämtliche Werke* XV, 57–8.

Neue Volkslieder von Brahms. 32 Bearbeitungen nach der Handschrift aus dem Besitz Clara
Schumanns. [Edited by Max Friedlaender.] [Nos. 1–28 for solo voice with piano accompaniment, Nos. 29–32 for mixed chorus.]
>
> Berlin: Deutsche Brahms-Gesellschaft, 1926 (*Publikationen*, No. 9).
> Republished in *Sämtliche Werke* XXVI, 191.

"Dem dunkeln Schoss der heil'gen Erde" aus Schillers "Lied von der Glocke" für gemischten
Chor. [Edited by E. Mandyczewski.]
>
> Leipzig: Breitkopf & Härtel, 1927 (*Sämtliche Werke* XXI, 155).

"Grausam erweiset sich Amor" (Goethe), Kanon für vier Frauenstimmen. [Edited by E. Mandyczewski.]
>
> Leipzig: Breitkopf & Härtel, 1927 (*Sämtliche Werke* XXI, 190).

Kleine Hochzeits-Kantate (G. Keller) für Sopran, Alt, Tenor, Bass mit Pianoforte. [Edited by
E. Mandyczewski.]
>
> Leipzig: Breitkopf & Härtel, 1927 (*Sämtliche Werke* XX, 226).

Spruch (Hoffmann von Fallersleben), Kanon für Stimme und Bratsche. [Edited by E. Mandyczewski.]
>
> Leipzig: Breitkopf & Härtel, 1927 (*Sämtliche Werke* XXI, 192).

Zu Rauch (Fr. Rückert), Kanon für Sopran, Alt, Tenor und Bass. [Edited by E. Mandyczewski.]
>
> Leipzig: Breitkopf & Härtel, 1927 (*Sämtliche Werke* XXI, 157).

[8] Deutsche Volkslieder, für vierstimmigen Chor gesetzt. [Edited by E. Mandyczewski.] [Num-
bered as 15–22 in *SW* to follow the 14 songs of 1864.]
>
> Leipzig: Breitkopf & Härtel, 1927 (*Sämtliche Werke* XXI, 144).

Zwei Giguen für das Pianoforte [in A moll, H moll]. [Edited by E. Mandyczewski.]
>
> Leipzig: Breitkopf & Härtel, 1927 (*Sämtliche Werke* XV, 53, 55).

Kadenz zu J. S. Bachs Klavierkonzert in D moll. [Edited by E. Mandyczewski.]
>
> Leipzig: Breitkopf & Härtel, 1927 (*Sämtliche Werke* XV, 101).

Kadenz zu L. van Beethovens Klavierkonzert in C moll, op. 37. [Edited by E. Mandyczewski.]
>
> Leipzig: Breitkopf & Härtel, 1927 (*Sämtliche Werke* XV, 120).

Zwei Kadenzen zu W. A. Mozarts Klavierkonzert in G dur (K. 453). [Edited by E. Mandy-czewski.]
Leipzig: Breitkopf & Härtel, 1927 (*Sämtliche Werke* XV, 102).

Kadenz zu W. A. Mozarts Klavierkonzert in D moll (K. 466). [Edited by E. Mandyczewski.]
Leipzig: Breitkopf & Härtel, 1927 (*Sämtliche Werke* XV, 105).

Kadenz zu W. A. Mozarts Klavierkonzert in C moll (K. 491). [Edited by E. Mandyczewski.]
Leipzig: Breitkopf & Härtel, 1927 (*Sämtliche Werke* XV, 109).

Zwei Präludien und Fugen für die Orgel. [Edited by E. Mandyczewski.]
Leipzig: Breitkopf & Härtel, 1927 (*Sämtliche Werke* XVI, 1, 7).

Thema mit Variationen aus dem B dur-Sextett [Op. 18, 2nd movement] für Clara Schumann
zweihändig gesetzt. [Edited by E. Mandyczewski.]
Leipzig: Breitkopf & Härtel, 1927 (*Sämtliche Werke* XV, 59).

Lieder der Ophelia (Ophelia's Lieder). Five Songs of Ophelia. To poems from Shakespeare's
"Hamlet" (German translation by Schlegel & Tieck). [Edited by Karl Geiringer.]
New York: G. Schirmer, 1935.

[Folk Songs for Women's Voices.] Edited with English words by Henry S. Drinker. [Contents:
27 folk songs, canons, and songs from the Hamburg *Frauenchor* Mss in the Drinker Collection (now at Smith College). Most are early variants of later standard versions published in the *Sämtliche Werke* XXI, XXVI. Three songs are otherwise unknown.] [Phila-
delphia?]: Henry S. Drinker, [n. d.] *(University of Pennsylvania Choral Series)*.

The first editions are:
[1] "Dein Herzlein mild du liebes Bild." [Composition by Brahms.]
[2] "Mein Herzlein thut mir gar zu weh" (Altes Liebeslied).
[3] "Übers Gebirg Maria geht." [Composition by Eccard.]

[Folk Songs for Women's Voices.] Siegfried Kross, "Brahmsiana: Der Nachlass der Schwestern
Völckers," *Die Musikforschung* XVII/2 (1964). [Contents: 20 folk songs edited from the
Drinker Manuscripts; most are early variants of later standard versions published in the
Sämtliche Werke XXI, XXVI. Three songs are otherwise unknown; they are republished
in Kross' *Der Chorsinger: Johannes Brahms, Volkslieder für Frauenstimmen* (Kassel:
Bärenreiter, 1965).]

The first editions are:
[1] "Ich hörte ein Sichlein rauschen" (Das Rauschen).
[2] "Ich stand auf hohen Berge" (Der Ritt zum Kloster).
[3] "Zu Strassburg auf der Schanz."

Folk Songs for Women's Voices arranged by Johannes Brahms. Edited by Vernon Gotwals and
Philip Keppler. [Contents: 28 folk songs, canons, and songs edited from the Drinker
Manuscripts at Smith College.] Northampton, Mass.: Smith College, 1968 (*Smith College
Music Archives* XV).
Reprinted, Kassel: Bärenreiter, 1970 (Siegmund Helms, ed. *Johannes Brahms, Volkslied-
bearbeitungen für Frauenchor*).

The first editions are:
[1] "Auf, auf, auf! Schätzelein" (Die Entführung).

[2] "Benedictus" (Canon). [Composition by Brahms.] [Facsimile of autograph (SSAT) previously published within Edward N. Waters' "The Music Collection of the Heinemann Foundation," *Notes* VII/2 (March 1950), 199–200. Smith College edition not reprinted by Helms.]

[3] "Es reiten drei Reiter" (Die Bernauerin).

[4] "Es stehen drei Sterne" (Das Lied vom eifersüchtigen Knaben).

[5] "Es steht ein Baum im Odenwald" (Der Baum im Odenwald). [Composition by J. Fr. Reichardt, 1781.]

[6] "Kein Feuer, keine Kohle" (Heimliche Liebe). [Two settings.]

[7] "Mein Herzlein thut mir gar zu weh!" (Altes Liebeslied.) [SSA variant of SSAA version published by Drinker (See above).]

[8] "Mein Schatz, ich hab es erfahren" (Dauernde Liebe).

[9] "Mein Schatz ist auf die Wanderschaft" (Während der Trennung).

[10] "Morgen muss ich fort von hier."

[11] "Sind wir geschieden" (Scheiden).

[12] "Wenn ich ein Vöglein wär'." [Composition by Brahms or R. Schumann?]

III. *Dubious Works Attributed to Brahms*

Opus 151. Souvenir de la Russie, Transcriptions en forme de Fantaisies sur des Airs russes et bohémiens, composées pour le piano à quatre mains, par G. W. Marks [pseudonym]. [Six books.]
Hamburg: A. Cranz, ca. 1852.
See O. E. Deutsch, op. cit., 268–9, 276–8, and Kalbeck, *Johannes Brahms*, I/1, 57.

Collection de Potpourris et Fantaisies des meilleurs Opéras, pour Piano, par G. W. Marks [pseudonym]. [Six books.]
Hamburg: A. Cranz, ca. 1852.
See Deutsch, ibid., 269, 276–8, and Kalbeck, ibid., 57.

Trio in A dur für Klavier, Violine und Violoncello. [Edited by Ernst Bücken and Karl Hasse.]
Leipzig: Breitkopf & Härtel, 1938.

The Ms, lacking a title page, and made by an unknown copyist, was discovered ca. 1924 by Erich Prieger of Bonn, who gave it to Ernst Bücken in 1924. The work was given its première in 1925 in the Rhenish Chamber Music Festival, and was subsequently edited by Bücken and Hasse for publication as a probable early work by Brahms. Its authenticity is doubted by such Brahms scholars as Karl Geiringer (See *Brahms; His Life and Work* [Garden City: Doubleday, 1961], 205–6.) The present location of the Ms is not known.

IV. *Arrangements of Works of Other Composers*

(In alphabetical order by composer)

AHLE, JOHANN RUDOLF. Choral aus der Kantate: "Es ist genug" von Johann Rudolf Ahle (1662).
Regensburg: Bosse, 1933 (*Zeitschrift für Musik* C/5 [May 1933], appendix).

BACH, JOHANN SEBASTIAN. Choral aus der Kantate Nr. 60: "O Ewigkeit, du Donnerwort" von J. S. Bach.
Regensburg: Bosse, 1933 (*Zeitschrift für Musik* C/5 [May 1933], appendix).

BACH, CARL PHILIPP EMANUEL. Sonaten für Clavier und Violine von C. Ph. E. Bach, Nr. 1 in H-moll, Nr. 2 in C-moll [Wq. 76, 78]. [Arranged anonymously.]
Leipzig & Winterthur: J. Rieter-Biedermann, [1864].

HÄNDEL, GEORG FRIEDRICH. [13] Duetti e [2] Terzetti von G. F. Händel.
Leipzig: Deutsche Händel-Gesellschaft, 1870, 1880 (*Georg Friedrich Händels Werke* XXXII).

_____. [6] Duette für Sopran und Alt von G. F. Händel mit Pianofortebegleitung von Johannes Brahms.
Leipzig: C. F. Peters, [1881].
Republished in *Georg Friedrich Händels Werke*, 2nd ed., XXXII, Nos. 15–20.

JOACHIM, JOSEPH. Ouvertüre zu Shakespeares "Heinrich IV" von Josef Joachim (op. 7), für zwei Pianoforte zu vier Händen gesetzt von Johannes Brahms.
Berlin: N. Simrock, 1903.

MOZART, WOLFGANG AMADEUS. Offertorium de Venerabili Sacramento ("Venite populi") für zwei 4-stimmige Gesangschöre und Orgel (2 Violinen ad lib.) von W. A. Mozart [K. 248a]. [Arranged anonymously.]
Wien: J. P. Gotthard, 1873.

SCHUBERT, FRANZ. Ellens zweiter Gesang aus Walter Scotts "Fräulein vom See" von Franz Schubert, op. 52, Nr. 2, für Sopran-Solo, [dreistimmigen] Frauenchor, und Blaseninstrumente gesetzt von Johannes Brahms.
Berlin: Deutsche Brahms-Gesellschaft, 1906 (*Publikationen*, No. 2).
Republished in *Sämtliche Werke* XIX, 153.

_____. Impromptu in Es, op. 90, Nr. 2, von Franz Schubert, Studie für die linke Hand.
Leipzig: Breitkopf & Härtel, 1927 (*Sämtliche Werke* XV, 44).

_____. Ländler für vier Hände (Original) nebst 11 von Johannes Brahms für vier Hände gesetzten Ländlern von Franz Schubert. (Series title: Franz Schubert Ländler für vier Hände.) [Edited by Georg Kinsky.]
Mainz: B. Schott, 1934.

_____. Three Songs by Schubert, orchestrated by Johannes Brahms: "Memnon," "An Schwager Kronos," "Geheimes."
London: Oxford University Press, 1932, 1933.

_____. Gruppe aus dem Tartarus by Schubert, arranged with orchestral accompaniment by Johannes Brahms.
London: Oxford University Press, 1937.

_____. Grosse Messe (Es) [D. 950] von Franz Schubert, für Clavier zu zwei Händen gesetzt. [Arranged anonymously.]
Leipzig & Winterthur: J. Rieter-Biedermann, 1865.

SCHUMANN, ROBERT. Quartett (Es) von Robert Schumann, Opus 47. Arrangement für das Pianoforte zu 4 Händen.
Berlin: Fürstner, 1887.

V. *Editions of Works of Other Composers*

(In alphabetical order by composer)

BACH, CARL PHILIPP EMANUEL. VI Concerti per il Cembalo, Nos. 1 & 5 [Wq. 43/1, 5] . . . C. P. E. Bach. [Edited anonymously.]
Hamburg: A. Cranz, 1862.

BACH, WILHELM FRIEDMANN. Sonate [in F] für zwei Claviere componirt von W. Fr. Bach. [Edited anonymously.]
Leipzig & Winterthur: J. Rieter-Biedermann, 1864.

COUPERIN, FRANÇOIS. Couperin Werke Herausgegeben von Johannes Brahms. Erster Theil. Clavierstücke. [Pièces de Clavecin, Livre I, II.]
Bergedorf bei Hamburg: H. Weissenborn, 1869, 1871 (Friedrich Chrysander's *Denkmäler der Tonkunst* IV).
Republished in revised edition (by Brahms and Chrysander), London: Augener Edition, 1888, 4 vols.

CHOPIN, FRÉDÉRIC. Die Mazurken und andere Werke für Pianoforte von Friedrich Chopin. [Edited anonymously.]
Leipzig: Breitkopf & Härtel, 1878–1880 (*Friedrich Chopins Werke* III, VIII, X, XIII).
Contents: Mazurken, III; Sonaten, VIII; Verschiedene Werke, X, Nos. 7, 8, 10, 12; Nachgelassene Werke, XIII, Nos. 3, 4, 5, 9, 14, 32.

MOZART, WOLFGANG AMADEUS. Requiem [K. 626] von W. A. Mozart.
Leipzig: Breitkopf & Härtel, 1877 (*Wolfgang Amadeus Mozarts Werke* 24/1; the Revisionsbericht by Brahms published 1886).

SCHUBERT, FRANZ. Drei Klavierstücke von Franz Schubert [Impromptus in es, Es, C von Mai 1828]. [Three books.]
Leipzig & Wintherthur: J. Rieter-Biedermann, 1868.

————. 20 Ländler für Pianoforte von Franz Schubert. [Edited anonymously.]
Wien: J. P. Gotthard, 1869.

————. [8] Symphonien von Franz Schubert.
Leipzig: Breitkopf & Härtel, 1884, 1885 (*Franz Schuberts Werke* I).

SCHUMANN, ROBERT. Scherzo und Presto passionato für das Pianoforte (aus dem Nachlasse) von Robert Schumann. [Two books.]
Leipzig & Winterthur: J. Rieter-Biedermann, Nov. 1866.
Republished in *Robert Schumanns Werke*, 1893 (see below).

————. Etudes Symphoniques en Forme de Variations pour Pianoforte par Robert Schumann. (Oeuvre posth. Suite de l'Oeuv. 13.) [Edited anonymously.]
Berlin: N. Simrock, [ca. 1873].
Republished, with Brahms' name, in *Robert Schumanns Werke*, 1893 (see below).

————. Neun nachgelassene Werke von Robert Schumann.
Leipzig: Breitkopf & Härtel, 1893 (*Robert Schumanns Werke* XIV, Supplement).
Contents: 1. Andante and Variations for 2 pianos, 2 violoncellos, horn; 2-4. Songs for solo voice with piano; 5. Song for 2 voices with piano; 6. Symphonic Etudes [2nd ed.]; 7. Scherzo for piano [2nd ed.]; 8. Presto for piano [2nd ed]; 9. Theme in E-flat for piano.

Bibliography

Albrecht, Otto E. *A Census of Autograph Music Manuscripts of European Composers in American Libraries.* Philadelphia: University of Pennsylvania Press, 1953.

Balassa, Ottilie von. *Die Brahmsfreundin Ottilie Ebner und ihr Kreis.* Wien: Kommissionsverlag Franz Bondy, 1933.

Brahms, Johannes. *Johannes Brahms im Briefwechsel mit Heinrich und Elisabet von Herzogenberg*, hrsg. Max Kalbeck, 2 Bde. (*Johannes Brahms Briefwechsel* I, II.) Berlin: Deutsche Brahms-Gesellschaft m. b. H., 1907. English translation as *The Herzogenberg Correspondence*, ed. Max Kalbeck, tr. Hannah Bryant. London: John Murray, 1909.

————. *Johannes Brahms im Briefwechsel mit Karl Reinthaler, Max Bruch, Hermann Deiters, Friedr. Heimveth, Karl Reinecke, Ernst Rudorff, Bernhard und Luise Scholz*, hrsg. Wilhelm Altmann. (*Johannes Brahms Briefwechsel* III.) Berlin: Deutsche Brahms-Gesellschaft m. b. H., 1908.

————. *Johannes Brahms im Briefwechsel mit J. O. Grimm*, hrsg. Richard Barth. (*Johannes Brahms Briefwechsel* IV.) Berlin: Deutsche Brahms-Gesellschaft m. b. H., 1908.

————. *Johannes Brahms im Briefwechsel mit Joseph Joachim*, hrsg. Andreas Moser, 2 Bde. (*Johannes Brahms Briefwechsel* V, VI.) Berlin: Deutsche Brahms-Gesellschaft m. b. H., 1908.

————. *Johannes Brahms Briefe an P. J. Simrock und Fritz Simrock*, hrsg. Max Kalbeck, 4 Bde. (*Johannes Brahms Briefwechsel* IX-XII.) Berlin: Deutsche Brahms-Gesellschaft m. b. H., 1917.

————. *Johannes Brahms im Briefwechsel mit Breitkopf & Härtel, Bartholf Senff, J. Rieter-Biedermann, C. F. Fritzsch und Robert Lienau*, hrsg. Wilhelm Altmann. (*Johannes Brahms Briefwechsel* XIV.) Berlin: Deutsche Brahms-Gesellschaft m. b. H., 1920.

————. *Letters of Clara Schumann and Johannes Brahms*, ed. Berthold Litzmann, 2 vols. London: Longmans, Green & Co., 1927.

————. *Johannes Brahms and Theodor Billroth: Letters from a Musical Friendship*, tr. and ed. Hans Barkan. Norman: University of Oklahoma Press, 1957.

————. *Johannes Brahms an Julius Spengel. Unveröffentliche Briefe aus den Jahren 1882–1897*, hrsg. Annemari Spengel. Hamburg: Gesellschaft der Bücherfreunde, 1959.

————. *Johannes Brahms und Fritz Simrock; Weg einer Freundschaft. Briefe des Verlegers an den Komponisten*, mit einer Einführung herausgegeben von Kurt Stephenson. (*Veröffentlichungen aus der Hamburger Staats- und Universitätsbibliothek*, Band 6.) Hamburg: Verlag J. J. Augustin, 1961.

————. *Johannes Brahms Sämtliche Werke*; Ausgabe der Gesellschaft der Musikfreunde in Wien, 26 Bde., hrsg. Eusebius Mandyczewski und Hans Gál. Leipzig: Breitkopf & Härtel, 1926–1928. Reprinted, Ann Arbor: J. W. Edwards, 1949. [The *Revisionsberichte* included in each volume contain general information about original editions, Mss, etc.]

————. *Johannes Brahms sämmtliche Werke* [Verzeichniss]. Nach dem Opus geordnet, mit Angabe der Verleger und Preise, sämmtlicher Arrangements und der Titel und Textanfänge aller Gesänge. Weimar: Eugen Eunike, Musikalienhandlung, 1878. [A 6-leaf sales pamphlet listing all works through Op. 73 and some WoO, with names of publishers and prices. Gesellschaft der Musikfreunde copy 3186/37 Cat. contains numerous annotations, especially dates, added by K. F. Pohl in pencil.]

————. *Verzeichniss der im Druck erschienenen Compositionen von Johannes Brahms.* Mit Angabe der Arrangements, Preise und Verlagsfirmen. Die Lieder und Gesänge (ein- und mehrstimmig) nach den Titeln und Anfängen der Texte alphabetisch geordnet. N.p., n. pub., n. d. [A 4-leaf sales catalog printed in Leipzig by Brückner & Niemann, ca. 1878.]

————. *Thematisches Verzeichniss der bisher im Druck erschienenen Werke von Johannes Brahms.* Nebst systematischem Verzeichniss und Registern. Berlin: N. Simrock, 1887.

————. *Thematisches Verzeichniss sämmtlicher im Druck erschienenen Werke von Johannes Brahms.* Nebst systematischem Verzeichniss und Registern. Berlin: N. Simrock, 1897, 1902, 1903, 1904, 1910.

————. *Vollständiges Verzeichniss sämmtlicher Werke und sämmtlicher Arrangements der Werke von Johannes Brahms.* Berlin: N. Simrock, 1897. [A 32-page pamphlet listing the Simrock editions.]

————. *Vollständiges Verzeichniss sämmtlicher Gesangswerke von Johannes Brahms.* Berlin: N. Simrock G. m. b. II., n. d. [1903?]. [Small leaflet listing works.]

————. *A Complete Catalog of Johannes Brahms' Works, Original and Arrangements.* London: Alfred Lengnick & Co., 1906. [A 4-p.l. and 68-p. pamphlet listing all published works, to ca. 1905, by the original publishers, without naming them in classified order by media. Lengnick was the British agent for Simrock. Included is an English translation of the biographical sketch published in Rieter-Biedermann's catalog.]

————. *Vollständiges Verzeichniss aller im Druck erschienenen Werke von Johannes Brahms.* Berlin: N. Simrock, G. m. b. H., 1908.

————. *Verzeichniss der im Druck erschienenen Compositionen von Johannes Brahms.* Vierte Auflage. Leipzig: P. Pabst, Oct. 1890. [A 32-p. pamphlet dealer's catalog listing all the works in print by the original publishers to 1890—through Op. 108 and some WoO.]

————. *Verzeichniss der Compositionen von Johannes Brahms nebst ihren Bearbeitungen aus dem Verlage von J. Rieter-Biedermann in Leipzig.* Leipzig: J. Rieter-Biedermann, 1905. [A 16-p. pamphlet containing a biographical sketch of Johannes Brahms and a publisher's non-thematic catalog of the Rieter-Biedermann publications. First issued in 1898.]

————. *Johannes Brahms, Verzeichnis seiner Werke, mit Einführung von Adolf Aber.* Leipzig: C. F. Peters, n. d. [1928?]. [A 23-p.l. and 49-p. pamphlet listing all (?) published works by Brahms, including various arrangements. Only Peters editions (including Rieter-Biedermann's) are identified by publisher and edition number.]

————. *Thematic Catalog of the Collected Works of Brahms,* enlarged edition. Edited with Foreword by Joseph Braunstein. [New York]: Ars Musica Press, 1956.

Deutsch, Otto Erich. "The First Editions of Brahms," *The Music Review* I/2, 3 (May and August 1940), 123–43, 255–78.

Drinker, Sophie. *Brahms and his Women's Choruses.* Merion, Pa.: The Author, 1952.

Ehrmann, Alfred von. *Johannes Brahms Weg, Werk und Welt.* Leipzig: Breitkopf & Härtel, 1933.

————. *Johannes Brahms Thematisches Verzeichnis seiner Werke. Ergänzung zu Johannes Brahms Weg, Werk und Welt.* Leipzig: Breitkopf & Härtel, 1933.

Anhang: Ergänzungen und Berichtigungen. Leipzig: Breitkopf & Härtel, 1952.

Gál, Hans. *Johannes Brahms, His Work and Personality,* tr. Joseph Stein. New York: Alfred A. Knopf, 1963.

Geiringer, Karl. *Brahms; His Life and Work,* tr. H. B. Weiner and Bernard Miall. Boston and New York: Houghton Mifflin Co., 1936.
Ibid., Second Edition. Revised and Enlarged, with a New Appendix of Brahms' Letters. Garden City: Doubleday & Co., 1961.

Gesellschaft der Musikfreunde. *J. Brahms Zentenar-Ausstellung.* Beschreibendes Verzeichnis zusammengestellt von Dr. H. Kraus, Dr. K. Geiringer, Dr. V. Luithlen. [Wien: Gesellschaft der Musikfreunde, 1933.]

Gotwals, Vernon. "Brahms and the Organ," *Music* (The A. G. O. and R. C. C. O. Magazine) IV/4 (April 1970), 38–55.

Gotwals, Vernon and Philip Keppler. *Folk Songs for Women's Voices arranged by Johannes Brahms.* Northampton: Smith College, 1968 (*Smith College Music Archives* XV).
Review by Donald M. McCorkle, *Notes* XXVI/3 (March 1970), 610–12.

Grasberger, Franz. *Johannes Brahms, Variationen um sein Wesen.* Wien: Verlag Paul Kaltschmid, 1952.

Hanslick, Eduard. *Musikalisches und Litterarisches* (Der "Modernen Oper" V. Theil). Berlin: Allgemeiner Verein für Deutsche Literatur, 1889.

Helms, Siegmund. *Volksliedbearbeitungen für Fraunenchor.* Kassel: Bärenreiter, 1970 (*Das 19. Jahrhundert*).

Hübbe, Walter. *Brahms in Hamburg.* Hamburg: Lütke & Wulff, 1902 (*Hamburgische Liebhaber-bibliothek*).

Kalbeck, Max. *Johannes Brahms.* 4 vols. in 8, Dritte Auflage. Berlin: Deutsche Brahms-Gesell-schaft m. b. H., 1912–1914.

Kross, Siegfried. *Die Chorwerke von Johannes Brahms.* Berlin u. Wunsiedel: Max Hesses Verlag, 1958. (2. Auflage 1963.)

Lübbe, Ingrid. *Das Schriftum über Johannes Brahms in den Jahren 1933–1958.* Unpub. Prü-fungsarbeit der Hamburger Bibliothekschule. Hamburg, 1960.
Mandyczewski, Eusebius. *Zusatz-Band zur Geschichte der K. K. Gesellschaft der Musikfreunde in Wien.* Wien: 1912.

May, Florence. *The Life of Johannes Brahms*, 2nd ed. revised by the author, with additional matter and illustrations, and an introduction by Ralph Hill. 2 vols. London: William Reeves, n. d. [ca. 1933?].

Musikbücherei der Hamburger Öffentlichen Bücherhallen. *Johannes Brahms. 7. Mai 1833—3. April 1897.* Hamburg: 1958 [Werkverzeichnis].

Orel, Alfred. "Ein eigenhändiges Werkverzeichnis von Brahms," *Die Musik* XXIX/8 (May 1937), 529–41.

————. *Johannes Brahms und Julius Allgeyer; Eine Künstlerfreundschaft in Briefen.* Tut-zing: Hans Schneider, 1964.

Pauls, Volquart. *Briefe der Freundschaft: Johannes Brahms—Klaus Groth.* Heide: Westhol-steinische Verlagsanstalt Boyens & Co., 1956.

Reimann, Heinrich. *Johannes Brahms.* 5. Aufl., durchgesehen und ergänzt von Bruno Schrader. Berlin: Schlesische Verlagsanstalt, 1910.

Schauffler, Robert Haven. *The Unknown Brahms.* New York: Crown Publishers, 1940.

Schneider, Hans. *Johannes Brahms Leben und Werk Seine Freunde und Seine Zeit.* Tutzing: Musikantiquariat Hans Schneider (Katalog 100), 1964. [A very valuable bibliographic catalog of Brahms autographs, editions, and Brahmsiana for sale in 1964.]

Simrock, N. *N. Simrock G. M. B. H. Jahrbuch.* Herausgegeben von Erich H. Müller. 3 vols.: I (1928), II (1929), III (1930–1934).

Simrock, N. *Verzeichniss des Musikalien-Verlags von N. Simrock in Berlin . . . Vollständig bis 1897.* [Has 2 entries for the Brahms *Thematisches Verzeichniss* on pp. 83 & 310.]

Spengel Julius. *Johannes Brahms, Charakterstudie.* Hamburg: Lütke & Wulff, 1898 (*Hamburg-ische Liebhaberbibliothek*).

Staats- und Universitätsbibliothek Hamburg. *Johannes Brahms Ausstellung* anlässlich der 125. Wiederkehr seines Geburtstages am 7. Mai 1833; Dokumente seines Lebens und Schaffens. Die Ausstellung und der Katalog wurden zusammengestellt von Dr. Gustav Fock und Dr. Kurt Richter. Hamburg: Staats- und Universitätsbibliothek, 1958.

Ziffer, Agnes, Bearb. *Katalog des Archiv für Photogramme Musikalischer Meisterhandschriften Widmung Anthony von Hoboken*, Teil 1 (Dritter Band, Museion Veröffentlichungen der Österreichischen Nationalbibliothek). Wien: George Prachner Verlag, 1967.

THEMATIC CATALOG OF THE
WORKS OF
JOHANNES BRAHMS

THEMATISCHES

VERZEICHNISS

SÄMMTLICHER

IM DRUCK ERSCHIENENEN WERKE

VON

JOHANNES BRAHMS.

NEBST SYSTEMATISCHEM VERZEICHNISS
UND REGISTERN.

N. SIMROCK IN BERLIN

1897.

Inhalt.

Thematisches Verzeichniss
der Werke von
JOHANNES BRAHMS.

Op. 1.
Sonate *(C dur)*
für das Pianoforte componirt und *Joseph Joachim* zugeeignet.

Leipzig, Breitkopf & Härtel.1853.

Verlags-№ 8833 [Pag. 3_31.] Preis 4 M.

Auch in: Pianoforte-Werke zu 2 Händen (Volksausg. № 131. Pr. compl. 9 M. n.) № 1.

Op. 2.
Sonate *(Fis moll)*
für das Pianoforte componirt und
Frau Clara Schumann
verehrend zugeeignet.

Leipzig, bei Breitkopf & Härtel.1853.

Verlags-№ 8834 [Pag. 2_27] Preis 3 M. 50 Pf.

Auch in: Pianoforte-Werke zu 2 Händen (Volksausg: № 131. Pr. compl. 9 M. n.) № 2.

Stich und Druck der Röder'schen Officin in Leipzig.

2

Op. 3.
Sechs Gesänge
für eine Tenor- oder Sopranstimme mit Pianofortebegleitung
componirt und *Bettina von Arnim* gewidmet.
Leipzig, bei Breitkopf & Härtel.1854.
Verlags-No 8835. [Pag. 3—15] Preis 2 M.

No 1. Liebestreu. *(Robert Reinick.)*
True love.

No 2. Liebe und Frühling. I. *(Hoffmann v.Fallersleben.)*
Love and Spring. (No 1.)

No 3. Liebe und Frühling. II. *(Hoffmann v.Fallersleben.)*
Love and Spring. (No 2.)

No 4. Lied aus dem Gedicht: „Ivan" *von Bodenstedt.*
Song.

No 5. In der Fremde. *(Eichendorff.)*
Among strangers.

No 6. Lied. *(Eichendorff.)*
Song.

Original-Ausgabe (ohne englischen Text.)
Einzeln No 1. (Liederkreis No 69) Pr. 50 Pf.
     2. („   No 201) Pr. 50 Pf.
     3. („   No 172) Pr. 75 Pf.
     4. („   No 202) Pr. 75 Pf.
     5. („   No 77) Pr. 50 Pf.
     6. („   No 182) Pr. 75 Pf.
Ferner in: Lieder (66) neuerer Meister (gr. 8°) (Volksausgabe No 352. Pr. compl. 5 M.) No 1—6.
Ausgabe für eine tiefere Stimme Pr. 2 M. 50 Pf. (In der transponirten Ausgabe steht No 1 und 4 in *C moll*, No 2 und 3 in
                                             G dur, No 5 in *D moll* und No 6 in *F dur.*)
Einzeln (Liederkreis) dieselben No und Preise wie Orig. Ausg.
Lieder Op. 3 und 7. Ausgabe für tiefere Stimme in Nummern 1884. No 1—6. Preise wie Orig. Ausg.
Six Songs for Tenor or Soprano composed with Pianoforte Accompaniment. For an upper voice. Translated
into English by *E. D'Esterre-Keeling.* Pr. 2 M. 50 Pf.
(Text s. oben)
Für Pianoforte mit Beifügung der Textesworte übertragen von
S. Jadassohn. Pr. 2 M. 50 Pf.
8607

Op. 4.

Scherzo *(Es moll)*

für das Pianoforte componirt
und seinem Freunde *Ernst Ferdinand Wenzel* zugeeignet.

Leipzig, bei Breitkopf & Härtel. 1854.
Verlags-№ 8836. [Pag. 3–13.] Preis 2 M.

Rasch und feurig.

Auch in: Pianoforte-Werke zu 2 Händen (Volksausgabe № 131. Pr. compl. 9 M. n.) № 3.
Für Pianoforte zu 4 Händen bearbeitet von FRIEDR. HERMANN. Preis 3 M.

Op. 5.

Sonate *(F moll)*

für das Pianoforte componirt
und der Frau Gräfin *Ida von Hohenthal* geb. Gräfin
von Seherr-Thoss zugeeignet.

Leipzig, Verlag von Bartholf Senff. 1854.
Verlags-№ 101. [Pag. 3–39.] Pr. 4 M. 50 Pf.

Allegro maestoso.

Andante. Der Abend dämmert, das Mondlicht scheint,
Da sind zwei Herzen in Liebe vereint
Und halten sich selig umfangen. *(Sternau.)*

Andante espressivo.   SCHERZO.
                             Allegro energico.

INTERMEZZO. (Rückblick.)   FINALE.
Andante molto.   Allegro moderato ma rubato.

Andante daraus einzeln. Preis 1 M. 50 Pf.
8607

Op. 6.
Sechs Gesänge

für eine Sopran- oder Tenor-Stimme
mit Begleitung des Pianoforte componirt
und den Fräulein *Luise* und *Minna Japha* zugeeignet.

Leipzig, Verlag von Bartholf Senff. Dcbr. 1853.

Verlags-Nº 94—100. [Pag. 3—23.] Preis 3 M.

Nº 1. Spanisches Lied. (Uebersetzt von *Paul Heyse*.)

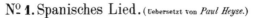

In dem Schatten mei-ner Lo-cken schlief mir

Nº 2. Der Frühling. (*J. B. Rousseau.*)

Es lockt und säu-selt

Nº 3. Nachwirkung. (*Alfred Meissner.*)

Sie ist ge-gan-gen, die Won-nen ver-

Nº 4. Juchhe! (*R. Reinick.*)

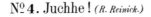

Wie ist doch die Er-de so schön, so schön!

N⁰ 5. „Wie die Wolke nach der Sonne" N⁰ 6. „Nachtigallen schwingen "(Hoffmann v.Fallersleben.)5

Poco Andante. (Hoffmann v.Fallersleben.)

Wie die Wolke nach der Sonne

Allegro non troppo.

Nach - ti - gallen schwingen lustig

molto stacc. e legg:

Einzeln: N⁰ 1 und 4. Pr.à 1 M.
N⁰ 2 „ 3. Pr.à 50 Pf.
N⁰ 5 „ 6. Pr.à 75 Pf.

Op. **7**.

Sechs Gesänge

für eine Singstimme mit Begleitung
des Pianoforte componirt
und *Albert Dietrich* gewidmet.
Leipzig, Breitkopf & Härtel.1854.
Verlags-N⁰ 8946. [Pag.3—13.] Preis **2** M.

N⁰ I. Treue Liebe. *(Ferrand.)*
True love.

Andante con espressione.

(Umfang)
dis - e

Ein Mägd - lein sass am Mee - res-strand, und
A mai - den sat by the lone sea - side, and

col Pedale

N⁰ II. Parole. *(Eichendorff:)*
The Huntsman.

Andante con moto.

(*c - gis*)

(5 Takte) Sie stand wohl am Fen - ster - bo - - gen und
Full lone-some and hea - vy - hear - - ted

col Pedale

N⁰ III. Anklänge. *(Eichendorff:)*
Fragment.

Andante molto. **p** mezza voce e legato

(*e - g*)

Hoch ü - ber stil - len Hö - - - hen stand
On yon - der hill ap - pea - - - ring

mezza voce

sempre legato

8607

6

Nº IV. Volkslied.
National Song.

Bewegt.

(e–g)

Die Schwäl - ble zie - het fort,
The swal - low flies a - way

Nº V. Die Trauernde. (*Volkslied.*)
The Mourning one.

Langsam.
p espressivo

(e–e)

Mei Mue - ter mag mi net, und kei Schatz han i net, ei wa - rum
My mo - ther loves me not

Nº VI. Heimkehr. (*Uhland.*)
Return Home.

Allegro agitato.

(e–gis) (5 Takte)

O brich nicht, Steg, du zit - terst sehr,
O break not, bridge, be - neath my tread

cresc. *sostenuto*

Original-Ausgabe (ohne englischen Text.)

Einzeln: Nº 1 und 2 (Liederkreis Nº 203 und 111) à 75 Pf.

Nº 3 — 6 à 50 Pf. (nicht im Liederkreis.)

Ferner in: Lieder (66) neuerer Meister (gr. 8º) (Volksausgabe Nº 352. Pr. compl. 5 M.) Nº 7—12.

Ausgabe für eine tiefere Stimme. Pr. 2 M.50 Pf. (In der transponirten Ausgabe steht Nº 1 in *E moll*, Nº 2 in *C moll*,
Nº 3 in *Fis moll*, Nº 4 in *Cis moll*, Nº 5 und 6 in *G moll.*)

Einzeln: Preise wie Original-Ausgabe.

Im Liederkreis dieselben Nummern und Preise wie Orig.-Ausg.

Lieder Op. 3 und 7. Ausgabe für tiefere Stimme in Nummern 1884. Nº 7—12. Preise wie Orig-Ausg.

Six Songs for one voice composed with Pianoforte Accompaniment. Transl. into English by E. D'Esterre-Keeling.

1884. Pr. 2 M.50 Pf.

(Text s. oben.)

Für Pianoforte mit Beifügung der Textesworte übertragen von S. Jadassohn. Preis 2 M.50 Pf.

Op. 8.
Trio
für Pianoforte, Violine und Violoncell.
Leipzig, bei Breitkopf & Härtel. 1859.
Verlags-№ 8953. Partitur [Pag. 2—55] und Stimmen. Preis 10 M.

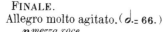

Für Pianoforte zu 4 Händen von FRIEDR. HERMANN. Preis 7 M.

Op. 9.
Variationen
für das Pianoforte
über ein Thema von ROBERT SCHUMANN.
Frau *Clara Schumann* zugeeignet.
Leipzig, bei Breitkopf & Härtel. 1854.
Verlags-№ 9001. [Pag. 3—19.] Preis 2 M. 50 Pf.

Auch in: Pianoforte-Werke zu 2 Händen (Volksausgabe №131. Pr. compl. 9 M. n.) № 4.
und in: Der Improvisator. Phantasien und Variationen für das Pianoforte. №10. Pr. 2 M. 50 Pf.

8

Op. **10.**
Balladen
für das Pianoforte.
Julius O.Grimm gewidmet.
Leipzig, bei Breitkopf & Härtel. 1856.
Verlags-№ 9226 [Pag. 3 _ 23.] Preis 3 M.

№ **1.** Nach der schottischen Ballade „*Edward*" (in *Herder's*
Andante. „Stimmen der Völker.") № **2.** Andante.
espress. e dolce

№ **3.** INTERMEZZO. № **4.** Andante con moto.
Allegro. *espressivo*

Auch in: Pianoforte-Werke zu 2 Händen (Volksausgabe №131. Pr. compl. 9 M. n.) № 5.
Einzeln: 1883. №1. Pr.75 Pf. №2. Pr.1 M. №3. Pr. 75 Pf. №4. Pr.1 M.50 Pf.
Für Pianoforte zu 4 Händen von FRIEDRICH HERMANN. Pr. 3 M.

Op.**11.**
Serenade *(D dur)*
für grosses Orchester componirt.
Leipzig, Breitkopf & Härtel. 1860.
Verlags-№ 5361. Part. 8? (Abklatsch) [Pag.1_217.] Pr.16 M.50 Pf.

Orchesterstimmen (2 Flöten, 2 Oboen, 2 Clarinetten, 2 Fagotte, 4 Hörner, 2 Trompeten, Pauken und Streichorchester) Pr. 21 M.
Einzeln: Viol. I. II., Bratsche, Vcell., C.Bass. Pr.
Für Pianoforte zu 4 Händen vom Componisten. Pr.7 M.50 Pf.
„ „ 2 „ „ von FRIEDR. HERMANN. Pr.4 M.50 Pf.
Menuett daraus für Pianoforte und Violine v. FRIEDR. HERMANN. Pr. 1 M.
Scherzo I.,II., Adagio und Menuett I für Pianoforte allein von L. STARK
(in: „Neue philharmonische Bibliothek für das Pianoforte. Ausgewählte Instrumentalsätze von Meistern
des 19. Jahrhunderts, vorzugsweise zum Studium des polyphonen und Partiturspiels bearbeitet und herausgegeben von L.STARK. Heft 6.) Pr. 3 M.50 Pf.

Op. **12.**
Ave Maria
für weiblichen Chor mit Orchester- oder Orgel-Begleitung.
Leipzig und Winterthur, J. Rieter-Biedermann. 1861.
Verlags-N° 165. 166. Partitur (ohne Orgel)[Pag. 3_15.] Pr. 2 M. 30 Pf.

Partitur (ohne Orgel) und Stimmen Pr. 5 M.
Chorstimmen Pr. 60 Pf.
Einzeln: Sopr. I. II., Alt I. II. Pr. à 15 Pf.
Orchesterstimmen (2 Flöten, 2 Hoboen, 2 Clarinetten, 2 Fagotte, 2 Hörner und Streichorchester) Preis 1 M. 80 Pf.
Einzeln: Viol. I. II., Bratsche, Violoncell und Contrabass Pr. à 15 Pf.
Orgelstimme Pr. 50 Pf.
Clavierauszug mit Gesang [Pag. 3_9.] Pr. 1 M. 50 Pf.
Für Pianoforte zu 4 Händen von Robert Keller. 1878. Pr. 1 M. 50 Pf.

Op. **13.**
Begräbnissgesang
für Chor und Blasinstrumente.
Leipzig und Winterthur, J. Rieter-Biedermann. 1861.
Verlags-N° 167. 168. Partitur [Pag. 3_13.] Pr. 2 M. 30 Pf.

Partitur und Stimmen Pr. 4 M. 50 Pf.
Chorstimmen Pr. 60 Pf.
Einzeln: Sopr. A. T. B. Pr. à 15 Pf.
Instrumentalstimmen (2 Hoboen, 2 Clarinetten, 2 Fagotte, 2 Hörner, 3 Posaunen, Tuba u. Pauken) Preis 1 M. 80 Pf.
Clavierauszug mit Gesang [Pag. 2_15.] Pr. 2 M. 30 Pf.
Für Pianoforte zu 4 Händen von Robert Keller. 1878. Pr. 2 M.

Op. **14.**
Lieder und Romanzen
für eine Singstimme mit Begleitung des Pianoforte.
Leipzig und Winterthur, J. Rieter-Biedermann. 1861.
Verlags-N° 169. [Pag. 2_23.] Preis 3 M.

N° 1. Vor dem Fenster. (Volkslied.)   N° 2. Vom verwundeten Knaben. (Volkslied.)

8607

№ 3. Murray's Ermordung.
(Schottisch, aus Herder's *Stimmen der Völker*.)
Con moto.

№ 4. Ein Sonett. (Aus dem 13. Jahrhundert.)
Langsam, sehr innig.

№ 5. Trennung. (*Volkslied.*)
Sehr schnell.

№ 6. Gang zur Liebsten. (*Volkslied.*)
Andante, con espressione.

№ 7. Ständchen. (*Volkslied.*)
Allegretto.

№ 8. Sehnsucht. (*Volkslied.*)
Andante.

Einzeln: № 1. Pr. 1 M. 40 Pf. № 2. 6. 8. à 70 Pf. № 3. 4. 5. 7. à 1 M.
Clavierübertragungen von Th. Kirchner. № 4. Pr. 1 M. 50 Pf.
№ 7. Pr. 1 M. 50 Pf.

Op. 15.

(Erstes) Concert (*Dmoll*)

für das Pianoforte mit Begleitung des Orchesters componirt.
Leipzig und Winterthur, J. Rieter-Biedermann. 1861.
In Stimmen Pr. 21 M.
Verlags-№ 815. Partitur in 8° 1875. [Pag. 1—171.] Pr. 15 M.

RONDO.
Allegro non troppo.

Orchesterstimmen (2 Flöten, 2 Hoboen, 2 Clarinetten, 2 Fagotte, 4 Hörner, 2 Trompeten, Pauken und Streichorchester) Pr.14 M.
Einzeln: Viol.I.II à 1 M., Viola 1 M.30 Pf.,Vcell.u.C.B.2 M.30 Pf.
Für Pianoforte allein Pr.7 M.
Für Pianoforte zu 4 Händen arr. vom Componisten Pr.9 M.
Für 2 Pianoforte arr.vom Componisten. Partitur 1875.Pr.9 M.
Für 2 Pianoforte zu 8 Händen bearbeitet v. Theodor Kirchner.1885.Pr.12 M.50 Pf.

Op.**16.**

Serenade

für kleines Orchester.
(Piccolo, 2 Fl.,2 Hob., 2 Cl., 2 Hörner, Bratschen,Violoncelli und Bässe.)
Neue,vom Autor revidirte Ausgabe.
N. Simrock in Berlin.1875.
Verlags-No 6129. Partitur [Pag.3_65.] Pr.12 M.

Die erste Ausgabe erschien Bonn 1860.

Stimmen (Piccolo, 2 Flöten, 2 Hoboen, 2 Clarinetten, 2 Fagotte, 2 Hörner, Bratschen,
Violoncelli und Bässe) Pr.20 M.
Einzeln: Bratsche Pr.2 M. Vcell. und C.B. 3 M.
Für Pianoforte zu 4 Händen vom Componisten. Pr.8 M.
Für Pianoforte zu 4 Händen mit Violine und Violoncell v. Friedr.Hermann. Pr.9 M.

12

Op. **17.**
Gesänge für Frauenchor
(Partsongs for Female voices, translated into English by Mrs. *Natalia Macfarren.*)
mit Begleitung von **2** Hörnern und Harfe.
(Auch zu blosser Pianofortebegleitung eingerichtet.)
Berlin, bei N. Simrock. 1862.
Verlags-N⁰ 6133. Partitur mit Clavierauszug [Pag. 3—19.] Pr. 3 M.

N⁰ **1.** „Es tönt ein voller Harfenklang" *(Ruperti.)*
"I hear a harp."
Poco Adagio, con molt' espressione.

N⁰ **2.** Lied v. Shakespeare.
Song from Shake-
speare's Twelfth Night.
Andante.

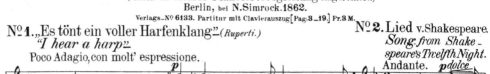

N⁰ **3.** Der Gärtner. *(Eichendorff.)*
Greetings.
Allegretto.

N⁰ **4.** Gesang aus Fingal. *(Ossian.)*
Song from Ossian's Fingal.
Andante.

Die erste Ausgabe ist ohne engl. Text.
Hörner- und Harfenstimme Pr. 2 M. 50 Pf.
Chorstimmen Pr. 2 M. 40 Pf.
Einzeln: Sopran I., II. und Alt Pr. à 80 Pf.
Für Pianoforte zu 4 Händen mit übergesetztem Text von Robert Keller. 1876. Pr. 3 M.

Op. **18.**
(Erstes) Sextett *(B dur)*
für **2** Violinen, **2** Violen und **2** Violoncelli componirt.
N. Simrock in Berlin. 1862.
Verlags-N⁰ 6202. Partitur in 8⁰ [Pag. 1—91.] Pr. 7 M. 50 Pf.

Allegro ma non troppo.

(TEMA CON VARIAZIONI.)
Andante, ma moderato.

SCHERZO. Allegro molto.   RONDO. Poco Allegretto e grazioso.   **13**

Stimmen Pr. 9 M.
Für Pianoforte zu 4 Händen vom COMPONISTEN. Pr. 8 M.
Für Pianoforte zu 4 Händen mit Violine und Violoncell von FRIEDR. HERMANN. 1876. Pr. 9 M.
Als Trio für Pianoforte, Violine und Violoncell bearbeitet von THEODOR KIRCHNER. 1883. Pr. 12 M.

Op. **19.**
Fünf Gedichte
für eine Singstimme mit Begleitung des Pianoforte.
(Translated into English by Mrs. *Natalia Macfarren*.)
N. Simrock in Berlin. 1862.
Verlags-No 7420. [Pag. 2_15.] Pr. 2 M. 50 Pf.

N<u>o</u> **1.** Der Kuss. (*Hölty.*)
The Kiss.
Poco Adagio.

N<u>o</u> **2.** Scheiden und Meiden. (*Uhland.*)   N<u>o</u> **3.** In der Ferne. (*Uhland.*)
Parting.   *Parted.*
Nicht zu langsam u. mit starkem Ausdruck.   L'istesso tempo.

N<u>o</u> **4.** Der Schmied. (*Uhland.*)   N<u>o</u> **5.** An eine Aeolsharfe. (*Mörike.*)
The forge.   *To an Aeolian harp.*
Allegro.   Poco lento.   Recit.

Die erste Ausgabe ist ohne engl. Text.
Einzeln in Ausgabe für hohe und tiefe Stimme: No 1.2.4. à 80 Pf. No 3.5. à 1 M.
(In der transponirten Ausgabe (1876) steht No 1 in *G dur*; No 2. 3 in *F moll*, No 4 in *C dur* und No 5 in *Fis dur*.)
Für Clavier allein übertragen (mit untergelegtem deutschen und englischen
Text) von ROBERT KELLER in: Brahms-Album. Band I No 1_5. [Pag 3_13.] (Bd. I compl. Pr. 5 M.)

8607

Op. **20.**

Drei Duette

für Sopran und Alt mit Begleitung des Pianoforte.

(Translated into English by Mrs. *Natalia Macfarren*.)

N. Simrock in Berlin. 1861.

Verlags-№ 6206. [Pag. 2—19.] Preis 3 M.

I. Weg der Liebe. (1ster Theil.) (Aus Herder's *Stimmen der Völker*.)

"Love will find out the way."

Allegro.

Ue — ber die Ber — ge, ü — ber die Wel — len,
O — ver the moun — tains, o — ver the wa — ves,

II. Weg der Liebe. (2ter Theil.)

Second Part of: "Love will find out the way."

Poco Adagio molto espressivo.

Den gor — di-schen Kno — ten, den Lie — be sich band, kann
Can skill dis-en-tan — gle the me — shes of love, or

p molto dolce ed espress.

III. Die Meere.

The two deeps.

Andante.

Al — le Win — de schla-fen auf dem Spie — gel der
All the winds are hush'd up — on the slum — be-ring

(4 Takte)

p dolce

Die erste Ausgabe ist ohne engl. Text.

Für Clavier allein übertragen (mit untergelegtem deutschen und englischen
Text) von Robert Keller in: Brahms-Album Band III. № 62—64.

[Pag. 4—13.] (Bd. III. Pr. compl. 5 M.)

Variationen

über ein eigenes Thema

für das Pianoforte.

N. Simrock in Berlin. 1861.

Verlags-№ 6203. [Pag. 2_13.] Preis 2 M.

THEMA (mit **11** Variationen).

Poco larghetto.

Für Pianoforte zu **4** Händen arr. von ROBERT KELLER. 1876. Pr. 3 M.

Op. **21**. № **2**.

Variationen

über ein ungarisches Lied

für das Pianoforte.

N. Simrock in Berlin. 1861.

Verlags-№ 6204. [Pag. 2_11.] Preis 2 M.

THEMA (mit **13** Variat. und Finale).

Allegro.

Für Pianoforte zu **4** Händen arr. von ROBERT KELLER. 1876. Pr. 3 M.

Op. **22**.

Marienlieder

für gemischten Chor componirt.

Leipzig und Winterthur, J. Rieter-Biedermann. 1862.

Heft I. Verlags-№ 216ᵃ Partitur in 8º [Pag. 2_9.] Preis 80 Pf.

Heft II. Verlags-№ 216ᵇ Partitur in 8º [Pag. 2_9.] Preis 80 Pf.

№ **1**. Der englische Gruss.   HEFT I.   № **2**. Maria's Kirchgang.

Con moto.

№ **3**. Maria's Wallfahrt.

Con moto.

№ 4. Der Jäger.

№ 5. Ruf zur Maria.

Zu № 4 vergl. Deutsche Volkslieder Heft II. № 7.

№ 6. Magdalena.

№ 7. Maria's Lob.

Stimmen zusammen für jedes Heft Pr. 1 M. 60 Pf.

Einzelne Sopran, Alt, Tenor, Bass à 40 Pf. pro Heft.

Op. 23.

Variationen

über ein Thema von Robert Schumann für Pianoforte zu vier Händen componirt.

Fräulein *Julie Schumann* gewidmet.

Leipzig und Winterthur, J. Rieter-Biedermann. 1866.

Verlags-№ 270. [Pag. 2—25.] Preis 3 M. 50 Pf.

THEMA (mit 10 Variationen).

Leise und innig.

Für Pianoforte zu 2 Händen bearbeitet von Theodor Kirchner. 1878. Pr. 3 M. 50 Pf.

Für zwei Pianoforte zu 4 Händen bearbeitet von Theodor Kirchner. 1885. Pr. 5 M.

Op. 24.

Variationen und Fuge

über ein Thema von Händel für das Pianoforte componirt.

Leipzig, Breitkopf & Härtel. 1862.

THEMA (mit 25 Variationen).   Verlags-№ 10448. [Pag. 3—23.] Preis 3 M. 50 Pf.

Auch in: Pianoforte-Werke zu 2 Händen (Volksausgabe № 131. Pr. compl. 9 M. n.) № 6.

Für Pianoforte zu 4 Händen bearbeitet von Theodor Kirchner. Pr. 5 M.

Op. **25.**

(Erstes) Quartett *(G moll)*

für Pianoforte, Violine, Bratsche und Violoncell.

Herrn Baron *Reinhard von Dalwigk* zugeeignet.

N. Simrock in Berlin. 1863.

Verlags-№ 6264. Partitur [Pag. 2—61] und Stimmen. Preis 13 M. 50 Pf.

Allegro.   **INTERMEZZO.**
Allegro, ma non troppo.

Andante con moto.   **RONDO ALLA ZINGARESE.**
                                  Presto.

Für Pianoforte zu 4 Händen vom COMPONISTEN. Pr. 9 M.

Für Pianoforte zu 4 Händen mit Violine und Violoncell v. FRIEDR. HERMANN. Pr. 13 M.

Op. **26.**

(Zweites) Quartett *(A dur)*

für Pianoforte, Violine, Bratsche und Violoncell.

Frau Dr. *Elisabeth Rösing* zugeeignet.

N. Simrock in Berlin. 1863.

Verlags-№ 6259. Partitur [Pag. 2—61] und Stimmen. Preis 13 M. 50 Pf.

Allegro non troppo.   **Poco Adagio.**

SCHERZO.   **FINALE.**
Poco Allegro.   **Allegro.**

Für Pianoforte zu 4 Händen vom COMPONISTEN 1872. Pr. 9 M.

Für Pianoforte zu 4 Händen mit Violine und Violoncell v. FRIEDR. HERMANN. Pr. 13 M.

8607

Op. 52.

Liebeslieder.

(Songs of love. Waltzes.)

Walzer

für das Pianoforte zu vier Händen (und Gesang ad libitum.)

Verse aus „Polydora" von *Daumer.*

(Translated into English by Mrs. *Natalia Macfarren.*)

N. Simrock in Berlin. Oct. 1869.

Verlags-№ 7024. Partitur [Pag. 3—47]. Preis 5 M. netto.

№ 1. (SOPRAN, ALT, TENOR und BASS.)

Im Ländler-Tempo.

№ 2. (S.A.T.B.)

№ 3. (TENOR und BASS.)

№ 4. (SOPRAN und ALT.)

№ 5. (S.A.T.B.)

№ 6. (S.A.T.B.)

Grazioso.

Op. 29.
Zwei Motetten
für fünfstimmigen gemischten Chor a capella.
Leipzig, Breitkopf & Härtel. 1864.
Nº I. Verlags-Nº 10636. Partitur in 8º [Pag.1_18.] Preis 2 M.
Nº II. Verlags-Nº 10637. Partitur in 8º [Pag.1_19.] Preis 2 M.

Nº I.
„Es ist das Heil uns kommen her."
CHORAL. FUGA à 5. Allegro.

Nº II.
Aus dem 51sten Psalm.
„Schaffe in mir, Gott, ein rein Herz."
Andante modto. Andante, espressivo. Andante.

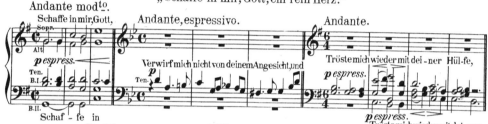

Partitur mit untergelegtem Klavierauszuge und Singstimmen in 8º
Nº I. Pr. 3 M. — Nº II. Pr. 3 M. (Partitur allein s. oben.)
Singstimmen einzeln: Nº I. Sopran, Alt, Tenor und Bass II. Pr. à 25 Pf., Bass I. Pr. 13 Pf., zusammen Pr. 1 M. 13 Pf.
Nº II. Sopran, Alt, Tenor, Bass I. u. II. Pr. à 25 Pf., zusammen Pr. 1 M. 25 Pf.

Op. 30.
Geistliches Lied
von *Paul Flemming*
für vierstimmigen gemischten Chor
mit Begleitung der Orgel oder des Pianoforte componirt.
Leipzig, Breitkopf & Härtel. 1864.
Verlags-Nº 10642. Partitur [Pag. 3_8.] Preis 1 M. 50 Pf.

Partitur und Singstimmen zusammen Pr. 2 M.
Partitur allein s. oben.
Singstimmen zusammen Pr. 50 Pf.
Einzeln: Sopran, Alt, Tenor, Bass Pr. à 13 Pf.

Op. **31.**

Drei Quartette

für vier Solostimmen (Sopran, Alt, Tenor und Bass)

mit Pianoforte componirt.

Leipzig, Breitkopf & Härtel. 1864.

Nº I. Verlags-Nº **10639.** [Pag. **3 _ 13.**] Preis **2 M. 25** Pf.

Nº II.   ,,   ,, **10640.** [Pag. **3 _ 11.**] Preis **2 M. 25** Pf.

Nº III.   ,,   ,, **10641.** [Pag. **3 _ 7.**] Preis **1 M. 50** Pf.

Nº **1.**

Wechsellied zum Tanze. *(Goethe.)*

Nº **2.**

Neckereien. *(Mährisch.)*

Nº **3.**

Der Gang zum Liebchen. *(Böhmisch.)*

Zu Nº 3 vgl. Op. 48. Nº 1. und Op. 39. Nº 5.

Partitur und Singstimmen Nº 1. 2. Pr. à 3 M. Nº 3. Pr. 2 M. Partitur einzeln s. oben.

Singstimmen zu Nº I.   Pr. 75 Pf. (Sopr., Alt, Tenor à 25 Pf.)

     ,,   ,, Nº II. Pr. 75 Pf. (S., A. à 13 Pf. T., B. à 25 Pf.)

     ,,   ,, Nº III. Pr. 50 Pf. (S., A., T., B. à 13 Pf.)

Op. 32.

Lieder und Gesänge

von *Aug. v. Platen* und *G. F. Daumer*
in Musik gesetzt für eine Singstimme mit Begleitung des Pianoforte.
Leipzig und Winterthur, J. Rieter-Biedermann. 1864.

Heft I. (Verlags-No 400ᵃ [Pag. 2_13.] Preis 2 M. 30 Pf.)
Heft II. (Verlags-No 400ᵇ [Pag. 2_13.] Preis 2 M. 30 Pf.)

HEFT I.

8607

N.º 5. *(Aug. v. Platen.)* HEFT II.

Allegro.

We - he, so willst du mich wie - der, hemmende

N.º 6. *(Aug. v. Platen.)*

Andante con moto.

Du sprichst, dass ich mich täusch - te, be - schworst es hoch und

N.º 7. *(G. F. Daumer, nach Hafis.)*

Con moto, espressivo ma grazioso.

Bit - te - res zu sa - gen denkst du, a - ber nun und

N.º 8. *(G. F. Daumer, nach Hafis.)*

In gehender Bewegung.

So steh'n wir, ich und mei - ne Wei - de, so lei - der

N.º 9. *(G. F. Daumer, nach Hafis.)*

Adagio.

Wie bist du, mei - ne Kö - ni - gin,
Ah, sweet my love, thou charmest me,

Einzeln: N.º 1. Pr. 1 M. 40 Pf. N.º 2. 3. 4. 5. 6. 7. 8. Pr. à 70 Pf. N.º 9. Pr. 1 M.
N.º 9 bis für tiefere Stimme *(Des dur)* mit deutschem und englischem Text (Englisch von *R. H. Benson.*) Pr. 1 M.
N.º 9 für Pianoforte allein von Theodor Kirchner. 1878. Pr. 2 M.

8607

Op. **33.**

Romanzen
aus *L. Tieck's* Magelone
für eine Singstimme mit Pianoforte componirt.
Julius Stockhausen gewidmet.
Leipzig und Winterthur, J. Rieter-Biedermann.
Heft I. II. 1865. Heft III. IV. V. 1868.
(Verlags-No 401 a. b. c. d. e.)
5 Hefte [I. Pag. 2_23. II. Pag. 2_23. III. Pag. 2_21. IV. Pag. 2_15. V. Pag. 3_19.] Pr. à 3 M.

HEFT I.

8607

HEFT II.

Nº 4.

Andante.

(*des-f*)
Lie-be kam aus fernen Landen
Love came forth from far-off places,

Nº 5.

Allegro.

(*es-g*)
So willst du des Ar - men dich
Will deign to be near me, Sir

Nº 6.

Allegro.

(*cis-fis*) (4 Takte)
Wie soll ich die Freu -de, die Won - ne denn tra - gen? Dass
O joy out of mea - sure, the hour of our greet -ing, my

HEFT III.

Nº 7.

Lebhaft.

(*e-g*) *poco f*
War es dir, dem die - se Lip - -pen beb - - ten,
'Twas for thee, for thee— my lips— were bur - ning,

con espressione

Nº 8.

Andante.

(*des-g*)
Wir müs - sen uns tren - nen, ge-
The hour of our par - ting, sweet

No 9.

Langsam.

No 10. Verzweiflung.
Despair.

HEFT IV.

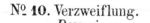

Allegro.

No 11.

Etwas langsam.

No 12.

Poco Andante.

N.° **13.** Sulima.

N.° **14.**

N.° **15.**

Original-Ausgabe (ohne englischen Text) **5 Hefte Pr. à 8 M.**

(Einzeln:) N.° 1. Pr. 2 M. 10 Pf. N.° 2. 5. 11 und 12. Pr. à 1 M. N.° 3 und 9. Pr. à 1 M. 70 Pf. N.° 4. 7. 8. 10. 13. 14 u. 15. Pr. à 1 M. 40 Pf.
1872. N.° 6. Pr. 2 M. 40 Pf.

Ausgabe für tiefe Stimme mit deutschem und englischem Text.
(Englische Uebersetzung von *A. Lang* und *R. H. Benson.*) 1875.
Fünf Hefte. Pr. à 8 M.

Einzeln (1877) zu denselben Preisen wie Originalausgabe.

(In der transponirten Ausgabe steht N.° 1. 4. 13 und 15 in *C dur*, N.° 2 und 10 in *A moll*, N.° 3 in *Ges dur*, N.° 5 in *D dur*,
N.° 6 in *G dur*, N.° 7 in *B dur*, N.° 8 in *Es dur*, N.° 9 in *Fis dur*, N.° 11 unverändert in *Fmoll*, N.° 12 in *E moll* und N.° 14 in *E dur*.)

Für Pianoforte allein von THEODOR KIRCHNER 1878.

N.° 3. Pr. 2 M.
N.° 5. Pr. 1 M. 50 Pf.
N.° 9. Pr. 2 M.
N.° 12. Pr. 1 M. 50 Pf.
N.° 14. Pr. 2 M.

Quintett

Op. 34.

für Pianoforte, zwei Violinen, Viola und Violoncell.

Ihrer Königl. Hoheit der Frau Prinzessin *Anna von Hessen* gewidmet.

Leipzig und Winterthur, J. Rieter-Biedermann. 1865.

Verlags-No 435. Partitur [Pag. 5—67] und Stimmen [40 Seiten] Preis 15 M.

Für Pianoforte zu 4 Händen bearbeitet von THEODOR KIRCHNER. 1884. Pr. 10 M.
Für Pianofrte zu 4 Händen mit Violine und Violoncell eingerichtet von FRIEDR. HERMANN. 1879. Pr. 12 M.
Für zwei Pianoforte: Op. 34 bis.

Sonate

Op. 34 bis

für zwei Pianoforte

nach dem Quintett Op. 34.

Ihrer Königl. Hoheit der Frau Prinzessin *Anna von Hessen* zugeeignet.

Leipzig und Winterthur, J. Rieter-Biedermann. 1872.

Verlags-No 678. Partitur [Pag. 5—64.] Pr. 9 M.

Themata siehe Op. 34.

Studien für Pianoforte.

VARIATIONEN

über ein Thema von Paganini componirt.

Leipzig und Winterthur, J. Rieter-Biedermann. 1866.

Verlags-No 436 a.b. Heft I. [Pag. 2—23] und Heft II. [Pag. 2—19] Pr. à 3 M.

HEFT I und II.

THEMA (mit 28 Variat. und Finale).

Non troppo presto.

Op. 36.

(Zweites) Sextett (*G dur*)

für **2** Violinen, **2** Violen und **2** Violoncelli componirt.

Bonn (Berlin) bei N. Simrock. 1866.

Verlags-No 6474. Partitur in 8º [Pag. 1—92.] Preis 7 M. 50 Pf.

Stimmen Preis **10 M.**

Für Pianoforte zu 4 Händen vom Componisten. Pr. 8 M.

Für Pianoforte zu 4 Händen mit Violine und Violoncell von Friedr. Hermann. 1876. Pr. 11 M.

Als Trio für Pianoforte, Violine und Violoncell bearbeitet von Theodor Kirchner. 1883. Pr. 12 M.

Op. 37.

Drei geistliche Chöre
für Frauenstimmen ohne Begleitung.

Leipzig und Winterthur, J. Rieter-Biedermann. 1866.
Verlags-N? 402. Partitur in 8? [Pag. 2 — 11] Preis 1 M.

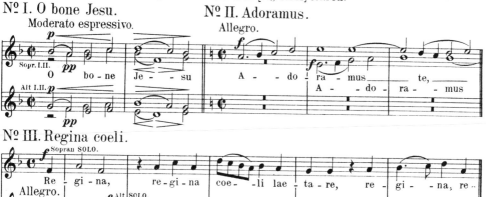

N? I. O bone Jesu.
Moderato espressivo.

N? II. Adoramus.
Allegro.

N? III. Regina coeli.

Solostimmen: Sopran, Alt à **15** Pf. = **30** Pf.
Chorstimmen: Sopran I., II., Alt I., II à 30 Pf. = 1 M. 20 Pf.

Op. 38.

Sonate
für Pianoforte und Violoncell.

Herrn Dr. *Josef Gänsbacher* zugeeignet.
N. Simrock in Berlin. 1866.
Verlags-N? 6476. Partitur [Pag. 2 — 24] und Stimme Preis 5 M.

Allegro non troppo.

Allegretto quasi Menuetto.

Allegro.

Für Pianoforte zu **4** Händen
arrangirt von ROBERT KELLER. 1875. Pr. 4 M. 50 Pf.
8607

Op. 39.
Walzer
für das Pianoforte zu vier Händen.
Dr. *Eduard Hanslick* zugeeignet.
Leipzig und Winterthur, J. Rieter-Biedermann. 1867.

Verlags-Nº 470. [Pag. 2–33.] Preis 4 M. 50 Pf.

Instructive Ausgabe in etwas leichterer Bearbeitung von J. Carl Eschmann. 1878. Pr. 4 M. 50 Pf.
Für Pianoforte zu 2 Händen vom Componisten. Pr. 3 M. Leichte Ausgabe vom Componisten. Pr. 2 M. 50 Pf.
Für Pianoforte zu 4 Händen mit Violine bearbeitet von Friedr. Hermann. 1880. Pr. 5 M. 50 Pf.
Für Pianoforte zu 4 Händen mit Violine und Violoncell eingerichtet von Friedr. Hermann. 1879. Pr. 5 M. 50 Pf.

Op.40.

Trio

für Pianoforte, Violine und Waldhorn
(oder Violoncell oder Bratsche.)
N. Simrock in Berlin. 1868.

Verlags-N⁰ **6503**. Partitur [Pag. 2–33] und Stimmen Preis 10 M.

Für Pianoforte zu 4 Händen arrangirt von ROBERT KELLER.1875. Pr. 6 M.

Op.41.

Fünf Lieder

für vierstimmigen Männerchor componirt.

Leipzig und Winterthur, J.Rieter-Biedermann. 1867.

Verlags-N⁰ 516. Partitur in 8⁰ [Pag. 2–19.] Preis 1 M. 50 Pf.

No **1.** Ich schwing' mein Horn in's Jammerthal. *(Altdeutsch.)* No **2.** Freiwillige her! *(Carl Lemcke.)*

Zu N⁰1 vgl. Op.43. N⁰3.

32

No 3. Geleit. *(Carl Lemcke.)*
Tempo di Marcia moderato.
mf
her! Von der

Was freut ei-nen al-ten Sol - daten? Drei
rf

No 4. Marschiren. *(C. Lemcke.)*
Im Marschtempo.
poco f
Jetzt hab ich schon zwei

No 5. Gebt Acht! *(Carl Lemcke.)*
Etwas gehalten.
mf
Jah-re lang in der verdamm-ten

f
Gebt Acht! Gebt Acht! Gebt Acht! Es harrt der Feind, der schlimm es
mf
Gebt Acht!   Gebt Acht! Gebt Acht! Gebt Acht! Gebt

Stimmen einzeln (Tenor I., II., Bass I., II.) Preis a 50 Pf. zusammen **2 M.**
Einzel-Ausgabe: No 1. Partitur Pr. **30** Pf. Stimmen Pr. à **15** Pf. = **60** Pf.
„ 2. „ „ **60** Pf. „ „ „ **15** Pf. = **60** Pf.
„ 3. „ „ **50** Pf. „ „ „ **15** Pf. = **60** Pf.
„ 4. „ „ **50** Pf. „ „ „ **15** Pf. = **60** Pf.
„ 5. „ „ **30** Pf. „ „ „ **15** Pf. = **60** Pf.

Op. **42.**
Drei Gesänge
für sechsstimmigen Chor a capella.
Hamburg, Aug. Cranz . (Wien, C. A. Spina.) 1868.
Verlags - No **5600 — 5602.** Partitur mit untergelegter Clavierbegleitung in 8º
[Pag. 3 _ 26] nebst Stimmen. Preis **5 M.**

No 1. Abendständchen. *(Clemens Brentano.)*
Langsam.

Sopr. *pp*
Alt I. II.
Hör; es klagt die Flö - te wie - der,
Tenor.
pp
Bass I. II. Hör; es klagt die Flö - te wie - der,

No 2. Vineta. *(W. Müller.)*
Con moto.
poco f espress.
Aus des Mee - res
(Mit selbständiger Pianofortebegleitung
ad libitum.)

No 3. Darthula's Grabesgesang. *(Nach Ossian von Herder.)*
Moderato, ma non troppo.

tie - fem, tie - fem Grun - de

Alt I. II.
p
Mäd - chen von Ko - la, du schläfst!

Stimmen (Sopr., Alt I u. II., Tenor, Bass I u. II.) Preis einzeln à **50** Pf.
Einzel-Ausgabe No 1. (Chor-Album II. No 21.) Partitur und Stimmen Stimmen einzeln à **30** Pf.
No 2. (Chor-Album No 6.) „ „ „ Pr. **2 M. 80** Pf. „ à **30** Pf.
No 3. „ „ „ Pr. **2 M. 50** Pf. „ à **30** Pf.
Für Pianoforte zu 4 Händen arrang. von C. Gurlitt:
No 1. Pr. **80** Pf. No 2. Pr. **1 M.** No 3. Pr. **1 M.**
8607

Op. 43.
Vier Gesänge
für eine Singstimme mit Begleitung des Pianoforte componirt.
Leipzig und Winterthur, J. Rieter-Biedermann. 1868.
Verlags-No 599ᵃᵇᶜᵈ [Pag. 2_19] Preis 3 M.

No 1. Von ewiger Liebe. (*Jos. Wentzig.* Nach dem Wendischen.)
Love is for ever.
Mässig.

(Umfang a–fis)   (4 Takte)
Dun-kel, wie dun-kel in Wald und in Feld!
Dee-per and dee-per o'er wood and o'er wold

No 2. Die Mainacht. (*Ludw. Hölty.*)
The may-night.
Sehr langsam und ausdrucksvoll.

(b–fes)
Wann der sil-berne Mond durch die Ge-sträuche blinkt,
When the sil-ve-ry moon glimm'reth through tangled boughs

No 3. Ich schell' mein Horn. (*Altdeutsch.*)
Durchaus nicht zu langsam und
ziemlich frei vorzutragen.
(Vorzugsweise Tenor.)

No 4. Das Lied vom Herrn von Falken-stein.
(Aus *Uhland's* Volksliedern.)
Allegro. Sehr kräftig.

(a–f)   Ich schell' mein Horn in's Jammer-thal,
p sotto voce

(c–g)   Es reit' der Herr von Falkenstein wohl

Zu No 3 vgl. Op. 41. No 1.

Einzel-Ausgabe No 1. Preis 1 M. 40 Pf.
No 1ᵇⁱˢ Dasselbe für höhere Stimme (*Cis moll*) mit deutschem und englischem Text (Uebersetzer *R. H. Benson.*)
Preis 1 M. 40 Pf.
No 2. Preis 1 M.
No 2ᵇⁱˢ Dasselbe für höhere Stimme (*Fis dur*) mit deutschem und englischem Text (Uebersetzer *R. H. Benson.*)
Preis 1 M.
No 3. Preis 70 Pf.
No 4. Preis 1 M. 40 Pf.
Für Pianoforte allein übertragen von THEODOR KIRCHNER. 1878.
No 1. Preis 2 M.
No 2. Preis 1 M. 50 Pf.
No 4. Preis 2 M. (1884)
Das Lied vom Herrn von Falkenstein (Op 43 No 4) für Männerchor und Orchester bearbeitet von
RICHARD HEUBERGER. 1879.
Partitur Preis 4 M.
Orchesterstimmen (2 Flöten, 2 Hoboen, 2 Clarinetten, 2 Fagotte, 4 Hörner, 2 Trompeten, 3 Posaunen und Streichorchester) Pr. 4 M. 50 Pf.
Einzeln Viol. I., II., Bratsche, Vcell., C. Bass à 80 Pf.
Clavierauszug mit Text. Preis 2 M. 50 Pf.
Singstimmen. Preis 1 M. 20 Pf.
Einzeln Tenor I., II., Bass I., II., à 30 Pf.

Op. 44.
Zwölf Lieder und Romanzen
für Frauenchor a capella
oder mit willkürlicher Begleitung des Pianoforte componirt.

Leipzig und Winterthur, J. Rieter-Biedermann. 1866.
Heft I. Verlags-No 474ᵃ Partitur [Pag. 2_17] Preis 2 M. 50 Pf.
Heft II. Verlags-No 474ᵇ Partitur [Pag. 2_15] Preis 2 M. 50 Pf.

HEFT I.

8607

Vier Lieder aus dem Jungbrunnen. *(P. Heyse.)*

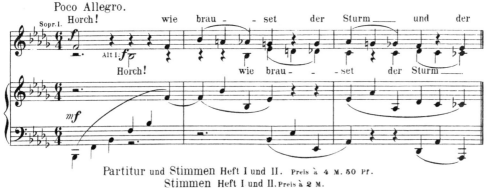

Partitur und Stimmen Heft I und II. Preis à 4 M. 50 Pf.

Stimmen Heft I und II. Preis à 2 M.

Einzeln: Sopr. I., II., Alt I. II. Preis à 50 Pf. für jedes Heft.

Die Einzel-Ausgabe in Nummern ist vergriffen.

Heft II. Nº 6. (Märznacht) findet sich abgedruckt in: Die Kunst des Gesanges von Julius Urban.

Practischer Theil III. Berlin bei Gustedt. S. 337.

(ohne Pianoforte-Begleitung)

8607

..

36

Op. 45.

Ein deutsches Requiem

nach Worten der heiligen Schrift
für Soli, Chor und Orchester (Orgel ad libitum) componirt.
Leipzig und Winterthur, J. Rieter-Biedermann. 1868.
Verlags-№ 592. Partitur [Pag. 1—191] Pr. 25 M.

I. (CHOR.)

Ziemlich langsam und mit Ausdruck. (M.M. ♩ = 80)

II. (CHOR.)

Langsam, marschmässig. (♩ = 60.)

8607

III. (Bariton - Solo und Chor.) (FUGE.)
Andante moderato. (♩=52.) (♩=54.)

Herr, leh-re doch mich, dich. Der Gerechten See-len sind in Got-tesHand
Lord, make me to know *But the righteous souls are in the hand of God*
Dieu, en-seigne moi *Car l'esprit du jus-te Dieu le gar-dera et*

sempre con tutta la forza

IV. (Chor.)
Mässig bewegt. (♩=92.)

Wie lieb-lich sind dei-ne
How love-ly is thy
Bien dou-ces sont tes de-

V. (Sopran - Solo und Chor.)
Langsam. (♪=104.)

Ihr___ habt nun Trau___-rig-keit,
Ye___ now are sor___-row-ful
Vous qu'af-fli-ge la___ dou-leur

(8 Takte)

8607

38 VI. (Chor.)

Andante. (♩ = 92.) p

Denn wir ha-ben hie kei — — ne blei-bende Statt,
Here on earth we have no_____ con-ti-nu-ing place,
Nous n'a-vous i-ci de_____ du-ra-ble ci-té   (207 Takte)

(FUGE.)
Allegro. (♩ = 100.)

Sieg! Herr, du bist wür-dig zu neh-men Preis und Eh — re und
Lord, thou art wor-thy of ha-ving praise and glo-ry and
Dieu, tu es di-gne de re-ce-voir la gloi-re, l'hon-

VII.(Schluss-Chor.)
Feierlich. (♩ = 80.) f

Se — — — lig sind die Tod — ten, die in dem
Bles — — — sed are the faith-ful, who in the
Gloire_____ à ceux qui meu-rent dans le Sei-

Orchesterstimmen:(Piccolo, 2 Fl., 2 Hob., 2 Cl., 2 Fag., 4 Hörner, 2 Tromp., Pauken, 3 Posaunen, Tuba,
Harfe und Streichorchester) Preis 24 M.
Einzeln: Violine I Pr. 1 M. 80 Pf. Violine II Pr. 1 M. 50 Pf. Viola Pr. 2 M. Violoncell u. Contrabass. Pr. 2 M. 30 Pf.
Chorstimmen: Preis 7 M. 60 Pf.
Einzeln: Sopran Pr. 1 M. 80 Pf. Alt, Tenor Pr. à 2 M. Bass Pr. 1 M. 80 Pf.
Solostimmen: Preis 60 Pf.
Textbuch: Preis 10 Pf. netto.
Clavierauszug mit Text in 4°. 1868. Preis 13 M. 50 Pf.
„ „ in gr. 8°. 1879. [Pag. 3–88.] Preis 6 M. netto.
„ „ in gr. 8°. Englische Ausgabe. Pr. 4 M. netto.
Partition pour chant et piano avec texte français, gr. 8°. Pr. 6 M. 40 Pf. netto.
Parties de chœur Preis 6 M. 40 Pf.
Soprano, Alto, Tenore, Basso Preis à 1 M. 60 Pf.
Clavierauszug zu vier Händen vom COMPONISTEN. 1869. Preis 10 M. 50 Pf.
„ „ zwei „ von THEODOR KIRCHNER. 1885. Pr. 8 M.

Op. 46.

Vier Gesänge

für eine Singstimme mit Begleitung des Pianoforte.

(Translated into English by Mrs. *Natalia Macfarren*.)

N. Simrock in Berlin. Oct. 1868.

Verlags-№ 7421. [Pag. 2—15] Preis 3 M.

№ 1. Die Kränze. (Aus Polydora von *Daumer.*)

The Garlands.

Ziemlich langsam.

Hier ob dem Ein - gang seid be - fe - sti - get, ihr Kränze, so be -

Here, o'er the door - way of her dwelling hang, ye garlands, all be -

p dolce

№ 2. Magyarisch. (*Daumer.*)

Magyar love - song.

Andante.

Sah dem ed - len Bild - niss in des Au - ges all - zu -

I have lost my heart with - in the star - ry depths of

p

legato

№ 3. Die Schale der Vergessenheit. (*Hölty.*) **№ 4. An die Nachtigall.** (*Hölty.*)

The cup of oblivion. *To a nightingale.*

Lebhaft, doch nicht zu rasch. Ziemlich langsam.

Ei - ne Scha - le des Stroms, Geuss nicht so laut der.

Oh, one cup of the tide *I pray thee, cease, in*

f p

Die erste Ausgabe ist ohne englischen Text.

Originalausgabe Pr. 3 M.

Einzeln in Ausgabe für hohe und tiefe Stimme: № 1. 3. 4. Pr. à 1 M. № 2. Pr. 80 Pf.

(In der transponirten Ausgabe (1876) steht № 1 in *H dur*, № 2 in *G dur*, № 3 und 4 in *D dur*.)

Für Clavier allein übertragen (mit untergelegtem deutschen u. englischen Text)

von ROBERT KELLER in: Brahms-Album Band I. № 6_9. [Pag. 14_24.]

(Bd. I. compl. Pr. 5 M.)

Op. 47.

Fünf Lieder

für eine Singstimme mit Begleitung des Pianoforte.

(Translated into English by Mrs. *Natalia Macfarren*.)

N. Simrock in Berlin. Oct. 1868.

Verlags-N?7422. [Pag. 2 — 20] Preis 4 M.

N?1. Botschaft. (Nach *Hafis* von *Daumer*.)

The message.

N?2. Liebesgluth. (Nach *Hafis* von *Daumer*.)

Consuming love.

N?3. Sonntag. (Aus *Uhland's* Volksliedern.)

Sunday.

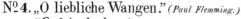

Nº 4. „O liebliche Wangen." *(Paul Flemming.)*
"O fair cheeks of roses."

Lebhaft.

O lieb - li - che Wan - gen, ihr macht mir Ver - lan - gen, dies ro - the, dies

O fair cheeks of ro - ses, where young love re - po - ses, my sen - ses en -

Nº 5. Die Liebende schreibt. *(Goethe.)*
To the beloved.

Non troppo lento.

Ein Blick von dei - nen Au - gen in die mei - nen, ein Kuss von dei - nem

A glance re - member'd that thine eyes have sent me, a kiss in hap - py

Die erste Ausgabe ist ohne englischen Text.

Originalausgabe Preis 4 M.
Einzeln in Ausgabe für hohe und tiefe Stimme. Nº 1_5. Pr. à 1 M.
(In der transponirten Ausgabe(1876)steht Nº 1 in *G moll*, Nº 2 in *Es moll*, Nº 3 in *As dur*, Nº 4 in *C dur* und Nº 5 in *Des dur*.)
Für Clavier allein übertragen (mit untergelegtem deutschen und englischen Text)
von ROBERT KELLER in: Brahms-Album Band I. Nº 10_14.[Pag.15_35] (Bd. I. compl. Pr. 5 M.)
Nº 3 (Sonntag) für Pianoforte in freier Uebertragung(mit vorgedrucktem
deutschen und englischen Text) von THEODOR KIRCHNER. 1882. Preis 1 M.50 Pf.
Dasselbe für Pianoforte frei bearbeitet von GUSTAV LANGE (in: Transcriptionen beliebter Lieder von
J. Brahms.) Op. 315 Nº 2. 1884. Pr.1 M.50 Pf.

Op. 48.
Sieben Lieder
für eine Singstimme mit Begleitung des Pianoforte.
(Translated into English by Mrs. *Natalia Macfarren.*)
N. Simrock in Berlin. Oct. 1868.
Verlags-Nº 7423.[Pag. 3_21] Preis 4 M.

Nº 1.Der Gang zum Liebchen. *(Böhmisch.)* | Nº 2.Der Ueberläufer. *(Aus des Knaben Wun-*
The watchful lover. | *The false love.* *derhorn.)*

Con grazia. | **Andante con moto.**

Es glänzt der Mond nie - der, ich soll - te doch | In den Garten wollen wir ge - hen,
The moon in high hea - ven the white clouds hath | *See the ro - ses blossoming yonder,*

Zu Nº 1 vgl. Op.31. Nº 3.

42

No. 3. **Liebesklage des Mädchens.** (Aus *des Knaben Wunderhorn*.)
The maid forlorn.
Etwas langsam.

(eis - fis) Wer se - hen will
Who - e'er would see

No. 4. **Gold überwiegt die Liebe.** (*Böhmisch.*)
Love betray'd for riches.
Poco Andante.

(e - g) Sternchen mit dem trü - ben Schein,
Oh thou star so dim and lone,

p legato
col Pedale

p espress.

No. 5. **Trost in Thränen.** (*Goethe.*)
Comfort in tears.
Andante.

(e - fis) Wie kommt's, dass du so traurig bist, da
Ah, why art thou so lone and sad, when

No. 6. „**Vergangen ist mir Glück und Heil.**"
"*Of ev'ry joy I am bereft.*" (*Altdeutsch.*)
Andante.

(d - g) Ver - gan - gen ist mir Glück und Heil
Of ev' - ry joy I am be - reft,

p dolce

p
d

Zu No. 6 vgl. Op. 62. No. 7.

No. 7. **Herbstgefühl.** (*A. F. von Schack.*)
Autumnal gloom.
Ziemlich langsam.

(d - es) Wie wenn im frost'-gen Windhauch tödt - lich
As when the Sum-mer's joys lie bu - ried,

pp sempre

Die erste Ausgabe ist ohne englischen Text.
Originalausgabe Preis 4 M.
Einzeln in Ausgabe für hohe und tiefe Stimme: No. 1. 5. 7. Pr. à 1 M. No. 2. 3. 4. 6. Pr. à 80 Pf.
(In der transponirten Ausgabe (1876) steht No. 1 in *G moll*, No. 2 in *B moll*, No. 3 in *A dur*, No. 4 in *D moll*,
No. 5 in *D dur*, No. 6 in *C dorisch* (1 Ton tiefer) und No. 7 in *A moll*.)
Für Clavier allein übertragen (mit untergelegtem deutschen und englischen Text)
von ROBERT KELLER in: Brahms-Album Band I. No. 15_21. [Pag. 36_48.] (Bd. I. compl. Pr. 5 M.)
No. 6 für gemischten Chor a capella s. Op. 62. No. 7.

Op. 49.

Fünf Lieder

für eine Singstimme mit Begleitung des Pianoforte.

(Translated into English by Mrs. *Natalia Macfarren.*)

N. Simrock in Berlin. Oct. 1868.

Verlags-No 6982. [Pag. 2 _15 resp. 17] Preis 3 M.

№ 1. Am Sonntag Morgen. (*Paul Heyse*, a. d. ital. Liederbuch.)

Last Sunday morn.

Andante espressivo.

№ 2. An ein Veilchen. (*Hölty.*)

To a violet.

Andante.

№ 3. Sehnsucht. (*Aus dem Böhmischen.*)

Wishes.

Langsam.

№ 4.Wiegenlied. (An *B. F.* in Wien.)
Lullaby.
Zart bewegt.

(es - es)

Gu - ten A - bend, gut' Nacht, mit Ro - sen be -
Lul - la - by and good night, with ro - ses be -

p

Ein zweiter Vers ist späteren Ausgaben zugefügt.

№ 5. Abenddämmerung. (*Adolf Friedr. v. Schack.*)
The twilight hour.
Ruhig.

(dis - fis) (6 Takte)

Sei will - kom - men, Zwie - licht-stun - de!
Gent-le twi - light, come, ___ sur-round me!

dolce p

p

Die erste Ausgabe ist ohne englischen Text.
Originalausgabe Preis 3 M.
Einzeln in Ausgabe für hohe und tiefe Stimme. № 1. Pr. 80 Pf. № 2_5. Pr. à 1 M.
(In der transponirten Ausgabe(1876)steht № 1 in *Cis moll,* № 2 und 5 in *D dur,* № 3 in *Fdur,*
und № 4 in *Ges dur.*)
Für Clavier allein übertragen (mit untergelegtem deutschen und englischen Text)
von Robert Keller in: Brahms-Album Band I.№ 22_26.[Pag. 49_62.]
(Bd. I. compl. Pr. 5 M.)
№ 2.(An ein Veilchen) für Pianoforte in freier Uebertragung mit vorgedrucktem deutschen
und englischen Text) von Theodor Kirchner. 1882. Pr. 1 M. 50 Pf.
№ 4.Wiegenlied. Paraphrase von Robert Keller f. Pfte. zu 2 Händen. 1873. Pr. 1 M. 80 Pf.
  „   „   „   „   „   „   „ 4   „   1877. Pr. 1 M. 50 Pf.
  „   „   „   „   „   „   „ 6   „   1877. Pr. 1 M. 80 Pf.
  „ Fantasie für Pianoforte von Gustav Lange. Op. 190ª Pr. 1 M. 80 Pf.
  „ Salon-Fantasie f. Pfte. von Joseph Löw. Op. 201ª Pr. 1 M. 50 Pf.
  „ Improvisation f. Pfte. von Franz Bendel. Op. 141. Pr. 2 M.
  „ Arrangement f. Pfte. und Violine von Friedr. Hermann. Pr. 1 M. 80 Pf.
  „   „ f. Pfte. und Flöte   „   „   „   Pr. 1 M.
  „   „ f. Pfte. Flöte und Violine (oder Pfte. und 2 Flöten)
     von Friedr. Hermann. Pr. 1 M. 80 Pf.
  „ Für Männerchor vierstimmig a capella bearbeitet von A. Zander.
Partitur Preis 1 M. Singstimmen Pr. 80 Pf. Einzeln: Tenor I., II., Bass I., II., Preis à 20 Pf.

Op.**50.**

Rinaldo.

Cantate von GOETHE

(The English version by *J. Powell Metcalfe.*)

für Tenor-Solo, Männer-Chor und Orchester componirt.

N. Simrock in Berlin. Aug. 1869.

Verlags № 326 (6985). Partitur [Pag. 5_141] Preis 22 M. 50 Pf. netto.

46

Auf dem Meere.
On the sea.

Orchesterstimmen (Piccolo, 2 Fl., 2 Ob., 2 Cl., 2 Fag., 2 Hörner, 2 Tromp., Pauken, 3 Posaunen u. Streichorchester) Pr. 24 M.
Einzeln: Violine I. Pr. 2 M. 50 Pf. Violine II und Bratsche à 2 M. Violoncell und Contrabass Pr. 3 M.
Chorstimmen Pr. 6 M. Einzeln: Tenor I., II., Bass I., II., Pr. à 1 M. 50 Pf.
Clavierauszug mit Text in 4° (fehlt) Pr. 12 M.
Clavierauszug mit deutschem und englischem Text in 8° [Pag. 7–86] Pr. 4 M. 50 Pf. netto.
Clavierauszug ohne Text zu vier Händen von Robert Keller. 1874. Pr. 9 M.
            "   "   " zwei   "   "   "   " in 8° Pr. 6 M.

8607

Op. 51.

Zwei Quartette

für **2** Violinen, Bratsche und Violoncell.

Seinem Freunde Dr. *Theodor Billroth* in Wien zugeeignet.

N. Simrock in Berlin. 1873.

No I. Verlags-No **7378**. Partitur in 8º [Pag. **2—39**] Preis 4 M. 50 Pf. netto.
No II. Verlags-No **7379**. Partitur in 8º [Pag. **3—43**] Preis 4 M. 50 Pf. netto.

Nº I. *(C moll.)*

Stimmen. Preis **7** M. **50** Pf. netto.
Für Pianoforte zu vier Händen vom Componisten. **1874**. Pr. 8 M.
„ „ „ „ „ mit Violine und Violoncell
von Friedrich Hermann. Pr. **10** M.

Nº II. *(A moll.)*

Stimmen. Preis **7** M. **50** Pf. netto.
Für Pianoforte zu vier Händen vom Componisten. Preis **8** M.
„ „ „ „ „ mit Violine und Violoncell
von Friedrich Hermann. Pr. **10** M.

Op. 52.

Liebeslieder.
(Songs of love. Waltzes.)
Walzer
für das Pianoforte zu vier Händen (und Gesang ad libitum.)

Verse aus „Polydora" von *Daumer.*

(Translated into English by Mrs. *Natalia Macfarren.*)

N. Simrock in Berlin. Oct. 1869.

Verlags-N.º 7024. Partitur [Pag. 3—47]. Preis 5 M. netto.

N.º 1. (SOPRAN, ALT, TENOR und BASS.)
Im Ländler-Tempo.

N.º 2. (S. A. T. B.)

N.º 3. (TENOR und BASS.)

N.º 4. (SOPRAN und ALT.)

N.º 5. (S. A. T. B.)

N.º 6. (S. A. T. B.)
Grazioso.

N.o 7. (SOPRAN oder ALT.)

TENOR.

Ein klei-ner, hüb-scher Vo — gel (Umfang c-fis) Wohl schön bewandt war es vor-
Was once a pret - ty ti - ny How sweet, how joy-ous dawn'd each

espress.

N.o 8. (S.A.T.B.)   **N.o 9.** (S.A.T.B.)

Wenn so lind dein Au — ge   Am Do — nau-
When thy glance is fond and   In wood em-

con 8

p dolce   p dolce   p dolce   cantando

N.o 10. (S.A.T.B.)

stran — de,   O wie sanft die Quel — le sich
bow — er'd,   Oh how soft yon murm'- ring stream

O wie sanft die Quel — le
Oh how soft yon murm'- ring

O
Oh   wie how

p dol.   con 8

p dolce

50

№ 11. (S.A.T.B.)

Nein, es ist nicht aus-zu-kom-men
No, there is no bearing with this

№ 12. (S.A.T.B.)

Schlosser auf, und ma-che Schlösser,
Locksmith, ho, a hundred padlocks,

Schlosser auf! und ma-che Schlösser,
Locksmith, ho, a hundred padlocks,

con 8

№ 13. (SOPRAN und ALT.)

Vö - ge-lein durchrauscht die
Bird in air will stray a-

poco f

№ 14. (TENOR und BASS.)

Sieh, wie ist die Wel - le
Bright thy sheen, oh lu - cent

p dolce

№ 15. (S.A.T.B.)

Sopr.Alt unis.

Tenor.
Bass.

Nach - ti - gall, sie singt so
Night-in-gale, thy swee - test

con 8

dolce

8607

№ 16. (S.A.T.B.)
Lebhaft.

Ein dun - ke - ler Schacht
Ah, love is a mine
Animato.

№ 17. (TENOR-SOLO.)
Mit Ausdruck.

(es - as)

Espressivo.

Nicht wand'-le, mein Licht,
Nay tar-ry, sweet-heart,

p dolce

№ 18. (S.A.T.B.)
Lebhaft.

Es be - bet das Ge - sträu - - che;
A tre - mor's in the bran - - ches,

Animato.

pp

pp

non legato

Singstimmen in 8° Text deutsch und englisch. Pr. 6 M. Einzeln (S.A.T.B.) Pr. à 1 M. 50 Pf.
Ausgabe mit Begleitung des Pianoforte Solo (zu 2 Händen) Pr. 3 M. 60 Pf. netto.
Für Pianoforte zu 4 Händen vom COMPONISTEN als Op. 52ᵃ Pr. 4 M. 50 Pf.
Für Clavier bearbeitet von THEODOR KIRCHNER. 1881. Pr. 4 M. 50 Pf.
Für Pianoforte zu 6 Händen von ROBERT KELLER. 1877. Heft I. II. Pr. à 2 M.
Für Pianoforte zu 4 Händen mit Violine und Violoncell von FRIEDR. HERMANN. 1875. Pr. 6 M.
Für Pianoforte mit Violine von FRIEDR. HERMANN. 1875. Pr. 4 M. 50 Pf.
Für Pianoforte und Flöte von FRIEDR. HERMANN. 1875. Heft I. II. Pr. à 1 M. 80 Pf.
Für Pianoforte, Flöte und Violine (oder Pianoforte und zwei Flöten)
von FRIEDR. HERMANN. 1875. Heft I. II. Pr. à 2 M. 50 Pf.
Für zwei Violinen von FRIEDR. HERMANN. (Partitur-Ausgabe) Pr. 3 M.

Op. 52ᵃ

Walzer
für das Pianoforte zu vier Händen
nach den Liebesliedern Op. 52.
N. Simrock in Berlin.

Verlags-№ 7528. [Pag. 2 – 81] Preis 4 M. 50 Pf.

Mit vorgedrucktem deutschen und englischen Text.
Themata siehe Op. 52.

Op. 53.

Rhapsodie

(Fragment aus GOETHE's Harzreise im Winter)

(Translated into English by *R. H. Benson*.)

für eine Altstimme, Männerchor und Orchester componirt.

N. Simrock in Berlin. Januar 1870.

Verlags - № 374 (7034). Partitur in 8º [Pag. 2 - 39] Preis 3 M. netto.

Orchesterstimmen (2 Fl., 2 Hob., 2 Clar., 2 Fag., 2 Hörner und Streichorchester) Pr. 3 M.

Einzeln: Violine I., II., Viola, Violoncello, Basso Pr. à 30 Pf.

Chorstimmen in 8º Pr. 1 M. 20 Pf. Einzeln: Tenor I., II., Bass I., II., Pr. à 30 Pf.

Clavierauszug mit Text in 4º (Translated into English by *R. H. Benson*.) [Pag. 2 - 15] Pr. 2 M. 25 Pf. netto.

(Die erste Ausgabe ist ohne englischen Text.)

Für Pianoforte zu 4 Händen von ROBERT KELLER (mit übergesetztem deutsch. Text) 1876. Pr. 2 M. 50 Pf.

Op. 54.

Schicksalslied

von *Friedrich Hölderlin*

für Chor und Orchester.

(Song of Fate.)

(Translated into English by Mrs. *Natalia Macfarren*.)

N. Simrock in Berlin. Dcbr. 1871.

Verlags - № 7177. Partitur in 8º [Pag. 1 - 60] Preis 4 M. 50 Pf. netto.

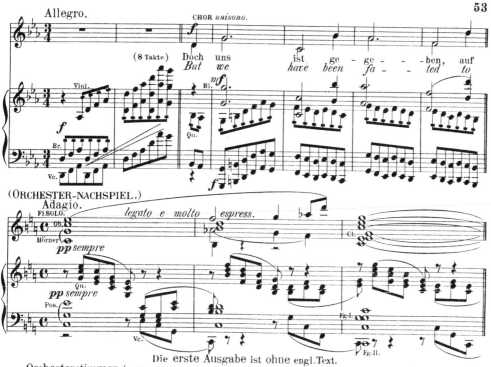

Die erste Ausgabe ist ohne engl.Text.

Orchesterstimmen (2 Fl., 2 Ob., 2 Cl., 2 Fag., 2 Hörner, 2 Tromp., 3 Pos., Pauken u. Streichorchester) Pr. 7 M. 50 Pf.
Einzeln: Viol. I. Pr. 80 Pf. Viol. II, Bratsche, Vcll., C.Bass Pr. à 50 Pf.
Chorstimmen in 8º. Pr. 2 M.
Einzeln: Sopr., Alt, Ten., Bass Pr. à 50 Pf.
Clavierauszug in 4º. Pr. 3 M. netto (fehlt.)
Clavierauszug in 8º. Neue Ausgabe mit deutschem und engl. Text [Pag. 3_21] Pr. 1 M. 50 Pf. netto.
Für Pianoforte allein mit vorgedrucktem deutsch. und engl. Text von ROBERT KELLER 1874.
Preis 1 M. 50 Pf. netto.
Für Pianoforte zu 4 Händen mit vorgedrucktem deutsch. und engl. Text von ROBERT KELLER 1874. Pr. 3 M.

Op. 55.

Triumphlied

(Triumphal Hymn)

(Offenb. Joh. Cap. 19.)

für achtstimmigen Chor und Orchester (Orgel ad libitum).

Seiner Majestät dem Deutschen Kaiser *Wilhelm I.* ehrfurchtsvoll zugeeignet.

N. Simrock in Berlin. 1872.

Verlags-Nº 7200. Partitur [Pag. 3_89.] Preis 18 M. netto.

Nº 1.

Mässig belebt.

(7 Takte)

CHOR I.
CHOR I.II. Lo — bet, lo-bet,
Glo — ry be to

Nº 3.
Lebhaft.

Lo — bet,
Glo — ry

(6 Takte)

BARITON SOLO und CHOR.

(SCHLUSSCHOR.)
Feierlich.

CHOR I.BASS.

Und ich sa-he den Him-mel
And be-hold, then the hea-vens

Ein Kö — — — — — nig al — ler Kö-ni-
A King _____ of Kings_ and Lord of

Orchesterstimmen (2 Fl., 2 Ob., 2 Cl., 2 Fag., Contrafag., 4 Hörner, 3 Tromp., 3 Pos., Tuba, Pauken und Streichorchester) Preis 24 M.

Einzeln: Viol.I.,II., Bratsche, Vcell., C.Bass Pr.à 1 M.

Chorstimmen Pr.10 M.40 Pf. (Einzeln 8 Stimmen à 1 M.30 Pf.)

Clavierauszug mit Text in 4º Pr.9 M. netto (fehlt.)

Clavierauszug. Neue Ausgabe mit deutschem und englischem Text.
In 8º [Pag.3—75] Pr. 4 M.50 Pf. netto.

Für Pianoforte zu vier Händen vom COMPONISTEN. Pr.9 M.

Op.56 ª
Variationen
über ein Thema von Jos. Haydn, für Orchester.

N. Simrock in Berlin. Januar 1874.

THEMA (mit 8 Variat.). Verlags-Nº 7395. Partitur in 8º [Pag.2—83.] Preis 9 M. netto.

CHORALE St. ANTONI.
Andante.

(FINALE.)
Andante.

Orchesterstimmen (Piccolo, 2 Fl., 2 Ob., 2 Clar., 2 Fag., Contrafag., 4 Hörner, 2 Tromp., Pauken (Triangel) und Streichorchester) Preis 18 M.

Einzeln: Violine I. Pr.1 M.50 Pf. Viol.II, Bratsche, Vcell. Pr.à 1 M. C.Bass Pr.80 Pf.

Für Pianoforte zu 2 Händen von LUDW. STARK. Pr.3 M.

Für Pianoforte zu 4 Händen von ROBERT KELLER. 1877. Pr.4 M.50 Pf.

Für zwei Pianoforte s.Op.56♭

Op. **56**♭

Variationen

über ein Thema von Jos. Haydn, für zwei Pianoforte.

N. Simrock in Berlin. Nov. **1873.**

Verlags-№ 7397. [Pag. 2—29] Preis 4 M. 50 Pf.

In Partitur gestochen, so dass zur Ausführung zwei Exemplare nöthig sind.

Themata und weitere Arrangements siehe unter Op.56ᵃ

Op. **57.**

Lieder und Gesänge

von *G. F. Daumer*

für eine Singstimme mit Begleitung des Pianoforte componirt.

Leipzig und Winterthur, J. Rieter-Biedermann. 1871.

Heft I. Verlags-№ 682ᵃ [Pag 2—15] Preis 3 M.

Heft II. Verlags-№ 682ᵇ [Pag 2—15] Preis 3 M.

HEFT I.

56 No 5. Agitato.

In mei - ner Näch - te Seh - - nen, so tief al -
Deep in my night - ly lon - ging, when none may

(fis-g) (4 Takte)

No 6. Sanft bewegt.

Strahlt zu - wei - len auch ein mil - des Licht
E - ver and a - non a kind - ly ray

(e-fis)

No 7. Etwas langsam.

Die Schnur, die Perl' an Per - le um
The pear - ly necklace shi - ning in

(fis-a)

No 8. Langsam.

Un - be - weg - te lau - e Luft, tie - fe
Not a breath in hea - ven stirs, Na - ture

(e-gis)

Original - Ausgabe:
Einzeln: No 1. Pr. 1 M. 40 Pf. No 2 und 6. Pr. à 70 Pf. No 3.4.5.7.8. Pr. à 1 M.
Ausgabe für tiefe Stimme mit deutschem und englischem Text (Ueber-
setzung von *R.H. Benson.*) 1879. Heft I. II. Pr. à 3 M.
Einzeln zu denselben Preisen wie die Originalausgabe.
(In der transponirten Ausgabe steht No 1 in *Es dur*, No 2 in *Des dur*, No 3 und 7 in *As dur*, No 4 in *D moll*,
No 5 in *Cis moll*, No 6 in *D dur* und No 8 in *C dur*.)
Für Pianoforte allein übertragen von THEODOR KIRCHNER. 1878.
No 2. Pr. 1 M. 20 Pf.
No 3. Pr. 1 M. 50 Pf.
No 6. Pr. 1 M. 20 Pf.

Op.**58**.

Lieder und Gesänge

für eine Singstimme mit Begleitung des Pianoforte componirt.

Leipzig und Winterthur, J. Rieter-Biedermann.1871.

Heft I. Verlags-No 683ᵃ [Pag 3 – 15] Preis 3 M.

Heft II. Verlags-No 683ᵇ [Pag 2 – 15] Preis 3 M.

№ **1.** Blinde Kuh. (Nach dem Italienischen v. *Aug. Kopisch*.)

Blind man's Buff.

HEFT I.

№ **2.** Während des Regens. (*Aug. Kopisch.*)

While the rain falls.

№ **3.** Die Spröde. (*Aus dem Calabresischen.*)

The Prude.

№ **4.** „O komme, holde Sommernacht!" (*M. Grohe.*)

"Sweet night of summertime."

8607

Original-Ausgabe:

Einzeln: No 1. 2. 3. 4. 7. Pr. à 1 M. No 5. 6. Pr. à 70 Pf. No 8. Pr. 1 M. 70 Pf.

Ausgabe für tiefe Stimme mit deutschem und englischem Text.

(Uebersetzung von R. H. Benson) 1879. Heft I. II. Pr. à 3 M.

Einzeln zu denselben Preisen wie die Originalausgabe.

(In der transponirten Ausgabe steht No 1 in E moll, No 2 in B dur, No 3 in G dur, No 4 in E dur, No 5 in Es moll,
No 6 in C moll, No 7 in D dur und No 8 in Fis moll.)

Für Pianoforte allein übertragen von THEODOR KIRCHNER. 1878.

No 3. Pr. 1 M. 50 Pf.

No 4. Pr. 1 M. 50 Pf.

No 5. Pr. 1 M. 20 Pf.

No 8. Pr. 2 M.

Op. **59.**

Lieder und Gesänge

für eine Singstimme mit Begleitung des Pianoforte componirt.

Englische Uebersetzung von Miss *E.M.Traquair.*

Leipzig und Winterthur, J. Rieter-Biedermann. 1873.

Heft I. Verlags-No 770a–d [Pag.2–21.] Preis 4 M. 50 Pf.n.

Heft II. Verlags-No 770e–h [Pag.8–14.] Preis 3 M. 60 Pf.n.

HEFT I.

No **1.** „Dämm'rung senkte sich von oben". *(Goethe.)*

Twilight.

No **2.** Auf dem See. *(Carl Simrock.)*

On the lake.

No **3.** Regenlied. *(Claus Groth.)*

Rainsong.

No **4.** Nachklang. *(Claus Groth.)*

Tears.

8607

60 № 5. Agnes. *(E. Mörike.)*

Agnes.

Con moto.

poco f *p*

Ro - sen-zeit, wie schnell vor - bei, schnell vor - bei
Love - ly time of ro - ses fair, ro - ses fair

(g - g)

poco f *p*

№ 6. *(G. F. Daumer.)*

Poco Andante.

(g - a) *grazioso* (5 Takte)

Ei - ne gu - te, gu - te Nacht
Dearest, when you say good night,

p

№ 7. *(Claus Groth.)*

Bewegt.

(e - g) (4 Takte)

Mein wundes Herz verlangt nach mil - - der Ruh, o
My wea-ry, ach-ing heart de - sires re - pose, breathe

f *poco f*

№ 8. *(Claus Groth.)*

Ziemlich langsam.

(b - g) *f* (3 Takte)

Dein blau - es Au-ge hält so still, ich bli - cke
While ga - zing in your blue eyes clear, I see in-

p *sf*

Original-Ausgabe mit deutschem und englischem Text.
Einzeln: № 1. 2. 4. 5. 6. 7 Pr. à 1 M. n. № 3. Pr. 1 M. 75 Pf. n. № 8. Pr. 75 Pf. n.
Ausgabe für tiefe Stimme mit deutschem und englischem Text. 1880.
Preise in zwei Heften und einzeln wie die Originalausgabe.
(In der transponirten Ausgabe steht № 1 in *B moll,* № 2 und 8 in *Es dur,* № 3 und 4 in *D moll,* № 5 in *E moll,*
№ 6 in *Fis moll* und № 7 in *Cis moll.*)
Für Pianoforte allein übertragen von Theodor Kirchner. 1878.
№ 2. Pr. 2 M.
№ 5. Pr. 1 M. 50 Pf.
№ 8. Pr. 1 M. 20 Pf.

Op. **60.**

(Drittes) Quartett *(C moll)*

für Pianoforte, Violine, Bratsche und Violoncell.

N. Simrock in Berlin. 1875.

Verlags-N⁰ **7702.** Partitur [Pag. **3 — 51**] und Stimmen. Preis **13 M. 50 Pf.**

Allegro non troppo.

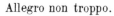

SCHERZO.
Allegro.

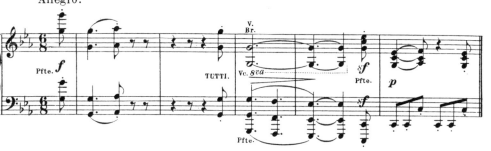

Andante.

FINALE.
Allegro comodo.

Für Pianoforte zu 4 Händen von Robert Keller. 1877. Pr. 8 M.
„   „   „ „   „ mit Violine und Violoncell
von Friedrich Hermann. Pr. 10 M.

Op. 61.
Vier Duette
für Sopran und Alt mit Begleitung des Pianoforte.
(Translated into English by Mrs. *Natalia Macfarren*.)
N. Simrock in Berlin. 1874.
Verlags-No 7452. [Pag. 3_21.] Preis 4 M.

No 1. Die Schwestern. (*Ed. Mörike.*)
The sisters.
Allegretto.

Wir Schwestern zwei, wir schö - nen, wir schö - nen, so gleich von An - ge -
Two sis - ters we, the fai - rest, the fai - rest, they call us ev'ry

No 2. Klosterfräulein. (*Just. Kerner.*)
The convent walls.
Andante.

Ach, ach, ich ar - mes Klo - ster - fräu - lein! O Mut - ter, was hast du ge -
A - las, the convent walls are drea - ry! Oh, mo - ther mine, what hast thou

No 3. Phänomen. (Aus dem *westöstl. Divan* von *Goethe*.)
Love hath not departed.
Poco Andante.

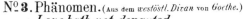

(4 Takte) Wenn zu der Re - gen - wand Phö - bus sich gat - tet,
When some low drif - ting cloud Phoe - bus en - cir - cles,

No 4. Die Boten der Liebe. (Böhmisch. Von *Josef Wenzig*.)
Envoys of love.
Vivace.

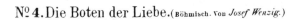

(5 Takte) Wie viel schön der Bo - ten
Thy en - voys I wel - come,

Für Clavier allein übertragen (mit untergelegtem deutschen und englischen Text) von ROBERT KELLER
in: Brahms-Album Band III. No 65_68 [Pag. 14_21]. (Bd. III. compl. Pr. 5 M.)

Op. **62.**

Sieben Lieder
für gemischten Chor (a capella.)

N. Simrock in Berlin. 1874.

Verlags-No **7453.** Partitur in 8° [Pag. **8_24**] Preis 4 M. netto.

N? **1.** Rosmarin. (Aus des Knaben Wunderhorn.)
Rosemary.
Gehend. (Andante.)

S.A.
Es wollt' die Jung-frau früh auf-steh'n, wollt'
At morning's prime went forth a maid, and

T.B.

N? **2.** Von alten Liebesliedern (Aus des Knaben Wunderhorn.)
"Before my fair maid's window"
Lebhaft.

Spa-zie-ren wollt' ich rei-ten, der
Be-fore my fair one's window one

N? **3.** Waldesnacht. (Aus dem Jungbrunnen von Paul Heyse.)
Gloom of woods.
Etwas langsam.

p dolce
Wal-des-nacht, du wun-der-küh-le,
Gloom of woods, re-fresh-ing cool-ness,

p dolce

N? **4.** „Dein Herzlein mild" (Aus dem Jungbrunnen von Paul Heyse.)
"Thou gentle girl"
Andante grazioso.

p dolce
Dein Herzlein mild, du lie-bes Bild,
Thou gen-tle girl, as fair as pearl,

p dolce

N? **5.** „All' meine Herzgedanken" (Aus dem Jungbrunnen von Paul Heyse.)
"Where'er I go"
Con moto. (Sechsstimmig, 2 Alte, 2 Bässe.)

p Tenor.
All' mei-ne Herz-ge-dan-ken
Where'-er I go or wan-der

Bass I.

Bass II.

N? **6.** „Es geht ein Wehen" (Aus dem Jungbrunnen von Paul Heyse.)
"I hear a sighing"
Ziemlich langsam.

Sopr.
Alt. *p*

Ten. *m.v.*
Es geht ein We-hen durch den Wald, die
I hear a sighing thro' the wood, the

Bass I. *p*

Bass II.
Es geht ein We-hen
I hear a sigh-ing

N? **7.** „Vergangen ist mir Glück und Heil" (Altdeutsch.)
"Of ev'ry joy I am bereft"
Andante.

Ver- -gangen ist mir Glück und Heil,
Of ev-ry joy I am he-reft,

Translated into English
by Mrs. *Natalia Macfarren.*

Singstimmen in 8° Pr. 4 M. 80 Pf. netto.
Einzeln: (Sopr., A., T., B.) Pr. à 1 M. 20 Pf.
Für Clavier allein übertragen (mit untergelegtem deutschen und englischen Text) von Robert Keller
in: Brahms-Album N? 1_6 in Band III N? 81_86
[Pag. 59_66]. N? 7 in Band I N? 20. [Pag. 45].
(Pr. pro Band 5 M.)

Zu N? 7 vgl. Op. 48. N? 6.

Op. **63**.
Lieder und Gesänge
für eine Singstimme mit Pianoforte.
Translated into English by Mrs. *Natalia Macfarren*.
Leipzig, C. F. Peters. 1874.

Heft I. Verlags-N° **6395ª** Edition Peters N° 1460ª [Pag. 3—23] Preis 1 M.50 Pf. netto.
Heft II. Verlags-N° **6395ᵇ** Edition Peters N° 1460ᵇ [Pag. 3—23] Preis 1 M.50 Pf. netto.

HEFT I.

N° **1.** Frühlingstrost. *(Max von Schenkendorf.)*
Comfort in Spring.
Lebhaft.

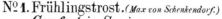

N° **2.** Erinnerung. *(Max von Schenkendorf.)*
Remembrance.
Innig.

N° **3.** An ein Bild. *(Max von Schenkendorf.)*
To a picture.
Etwas langsam.

N° **4.** An die Tauben. *(Max von Schenkendorf.)*
To a Dove.
Sehr lebhaft.

No 5. Junge Lieder. I. *(F. S.)*
Youthful lays. I.
Lebhaft.

No 6. Junge Lieder. II. *(F. S.)*
Youthful lays. II.
Zart bewegt.

Mei-ne Lie - - -be ist grün__
Like a blos - - soming li - -

Wenn um den Hollunder der
When twilight's soft breezes the

No 7. Heimweh. I. *(Claus Groth.)*
Far from home. I.
Zart bewegt.

Wie traulich war das Fleck - chen, wo mei - ne Wie-ge
Oh cottage dear and home - ly, where once my cra-dle

No 8. Heimweh. II. *(Claus Groth.)*
Far from home. II.
Etwas langsam.

O wüsst' · ich doch den Weg zu - rück, den
Oh that I might re - trace the way, the

No 9. Heimweh. III. *(Claus Groth.)*
Far from home. III.
Etwas langsam.

Ich sah als Kna - be Blu - men blüh'n__ ich weiss nicht
The flow'rs that bloom'd for me, a child, their wond'rous

In die Edition Peters aufgenommen. kl. 4º.
Ausgabe für tiefe Stimme. Heft I. II. Preis à 1 M. 50 Pf. netto.
(In der transponirten Ausgabe steht No 1, 3 und 9 in *F dur*, No 2 und 4 in *A dur*, No 5 in *D dur*,
No 6 in *H dur*, No 7 in *E dur* und No 8 in *Cis dur*.)

66

Op.**64**.
Quartette
für vier Solostimmen mit Pianoforte.
Leipzig, C.F.Peters. 1874.
Verlags-No 5705. Edition Peters No 1461. Partitur kl.4º [Pag. **2 — 27**.]
Preis **2 M. 40** Pf. netto.

Nº **1.** An die Heimath. *(C.O. Sternau.)*
Bewegt, doch nicht zu schnell.

Nº **2.** Der Abend. *(Fr. Schiller.)*
Ruhig.

Nº **3.** Fragen. *(G.F. Daumer.)*
Andante con moto.

In die Edition Peters aufgenommen.
Stimmen (Sopran, Alt, Tenor, Bass) in 8º Preis **2** M. **40** Pf. netto.

8607

Op. 65.
Neue Liebeslieder.
WALZER
für vier Singstimmen und Pianoforte zu vier Händen.
Verse aus „Polydora" von *Daumer.*
(New Songs of Love. Waltzes.)
(Translated into English by Mrs. *Natalia Macfarren.*)
N. Simrock in Berlin. 1875.
Verlags-N° 7670. Partitur [Pag. 3—41] Pr. 4 M. 50 Pf. netto.

68

Singstimmen (S.,A.,T.,B.) in 8º Pr. 4 M. Einzeln à 1 M.
Bearbeitung für Pianoforte zu 4 Händen ohne Gesang vom Componisten Op 65ª 1877.[Pag.2—27] Pr.4 M.50 Pf.
Mit vorgedrucktem deutschen und englischen Text.
Für Clavier (zu 2 Händen) bearbeitet von THEODOR KIRCHNER. 1881. Pr.4 M.50 Pf.

8607

Op. **66.**

Fünf Duette

für Sopran und Alt mit Begleitung des Pianoforte.

(Translated into English by Mrs. *Natalia Macfarren.*)

N. Simrock in Berlin. 1875.

Verlags-N? 7708. [Pag. 2 – 19] Preis 4 M.

N? **1.** Klänge. I. *(Claus Groth.)*

True lover's heart.

Andante.

Aus der Er - de quel - len Blu - men, aus der
From the kind-ly earth spring flow-ers, from the

N? **2.** Klänge. II. *(Claus Groth.)*

True lover's plaint.

Andante.

Wenn ein mü - der Leib be - -gra - - ben,
When a wea-ry heart re- -po- - ses,

N? **3.** Am Strande. *(Hermann Hölty.)*

By Summer Sea.

Ruhig.

dolce

Es spre - chen und bli - cken die Wel - - len mit
Bright waves, ye are glan-cing and murm'-ring, with

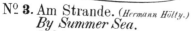
dolce

N? **4.** Jägerlied. *(Carl Candidus.)*

The Huntsman.

Lebhaft.

Sopr.

Jä - ger, was jagst du die Hä - - se - lein, die
Huntsman, why cha-sest the gen - tle roe, the

70 **№ 5. „Hüt' du dich."** (Aus des Knaben Wunderhorn.)
Beware! (Words slighty altered from Longfellow.)

Lebhaft, heimlich und schalkhaft.   m.v.

Ich weiss ein Mäd' - lein hübsch und
I know a mai - den fair to

Die erste Ausgabe ist ohne englischen Text.
Fur Clavier allein übertragen (mit untergelegtem deutschen und englischen Text) von ROBERT KELLER
in: Brahms-Album Band III. № 69_73. [Pag. 22_33] (Bd. III. compl. Pr. 5 M.)

Op.67.

Quartett

(№ III. *B dur*)

für zwei Violinen, Bratsche und Violoncell.
Seinem Freunde Professor *Th.W.Engelmann* in Utrecht zugeeignet.
N. Simrock in Berlin. 1876.

Verlags-№ 7892. Partitur in 8º [Pag. 2_39] Preis 4 M.50 Pf. n.

Vivace.

Andante.

Agitato.(Allegretto non troppo.)

Poco Allegretto con variazioni.

Doppio Movimento.

Stimmen Preis 7 M.50 Pf. n.
Für Pianoforte zu 4 Händen vom Componisten. [Pag. 2_55]1877.Pr. 8 M.
Für Pianoforte zu 4 Händen mit Violine u.Violoncell von FRIEDR.HERMANN Pr.10 M.

Op. **68.**

(Erste) Symphonie (*C moll*)

für grosses Orchester.

N. Simrock in Berlin. 1877.

Verlags-No. **7957.** Partitur [Pag. **3**—**100**] Preis **80** M. netto.

Orchesterstimmen (2 Fl., 2 Ob., 2 Cl., 2 Fag., Contrafag., 4 Hörner, 2 Tromp., 3 Posaunen, Pauken und Streichorchester) Preis 36 M.

Eineln: Viol. I., II., Bratsche Pr. à 3 M. Vcll. Pr. 2 M. 50 Pf. Contrabass Preis 2 M.

Für Pianoforte zu 4 Händen vom Componisten. 1878. [Pag. 2 — 67] Pr. 12 M.

Für zwei Pianoforte zu 8 Händen von ROBERT KELLER. 1878. Pr. 15 M.

Für Pianoforte zu 2 Händen von ROBERT KELLER. 1880. Pr. 8 M.

8607

Op. 69.
Neun Gesänge
für eine Singstimme mit Begleitung des Pianoforte.

(Translation into English by Mrs. *Natalia Macfarren*.)

N. Simrock in Berlin. 1877.

Heft I. Verlags-Nº 7951 [Pag. 3—19] Preis 4 M.
Heft II. Verlags-Nº 7952 [Pag. 3—22] Preis 4 M.

HEFT I.

Nº 1. Klage. *(Jos. Wenzig. Aus dem Böhmischen.)*
Lament.

Nº 2. Klage. *(Jos. Wenzig. Slowakisch.)*
Complaint.

Nº 3. Abschied. *(Jos. Wenzig. Böhmisch.)*
Parting.

Nº 4. Des Liebsten Schwur. *(Jos. Wenzig. Aus dem Böhmischen.)*
The lover's vow.

Nº 5. Tambourliedchen. *(Karl Candidus.)*
Drummer's song.

№ 6. Vom Strande. *(Jos. v. Eichendorff.*
On the shore. *Nach dem Spanischen.)*
Bewegt. (Con moto.)

№ 7. Ueber die See. *(Carl Lemcke.)*
Over the sea.
Andante.

№ 8. Salome. *(Gottfried Keller.)*
Salome.
Sehr lebhaft.

№ 9. Mädchenfluch. *(Siegfried Kapper. Nach dem Serbischen.)*
Maiden's curses.
Belebt.

Die erste Ausgabe ist ohne englischen Text.
Einzeln in Ausgabe für hohe und tiefe Stimme. № 1 . 2 . 5 . 8 . Pr. à 1 M.
№ 3 . 7. Pr. à 80 Pf. № 4 . 6 . 9. Pr. à 1 M. 50 Pf.
(In der transponirten Ausgabe (1879) steht № 1 in *C dur*, № 2 in *H moll*, № 3 u. 5 in *F dur*, № 4 in *G dur*, № 6 u. 9
in *F moll*, № 7 in *Cis moll* und № 8 in *A dur*.)
Für Clavier allein übertragen (mit untergelegtem deutschen und englischen Text) von ROBERT KELLER
in: Brahms-Album Band I. № 27_ 35. [Pag. 63_83] (Ed. I. compl. Pr. 5 M.)
№ 3 (Abschied) und № 4 (Des Liebsten Schwur) für Pianoforte in freier Uebertragung (mit vorgedrucktem deutschen und englischen Text) von THEOD. KIRCHNER. 1882. № 3. Pr. 1 M. № 4. Pr. 1 M. 50 Pf.

74

Op. **70.**

Vier Gesänge

für eine Singstimme mit Begleitung des Pianoforte.

(Translated into English by Mrs. *Natalia Macfarren.*)

N. Simrock in Berlin. 1877.

Verlags-Nº 7953. [Pag. 3 _ 15.] Preis **4 M.**

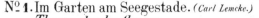

Nº **1.** Im Garten am Seegestade. *(Carl Lemcke.)*

The garden by the sea.

Traurig, doch nicht zu langsam.

Nº **2.** Lerchengesang. *(Karl Candidus.)*

The skylark's song.

Andante espressivo.

Nº **3.** Serenade. *(Goethe.)*

Question.

Grazioso.

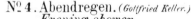

Nº **4.** Abendregen. *(Gottfried Keller.)*

Evening shower.

Ruhig.

Die erste Ausgabe ist ohne englischen Text.

Nº 4. (Abendregen) erschien zuerst in: Blätter für Hausmusik, herausgegeben von E.W. Fritzsch.

Classe A. Gesangsmusik. Jahrg. I. Heft I. 1. October 1875. S. 6_8.

Einzeln in Ausgabe für hohe und tiefe Stimme. Nº 1.2 Pr. à 1 M. Nº 3 Pr. 80 Pf. Nº 4. Pr. 1 M. 50 Pf.

(In der transponirten Ausgabe (1879) steht Nº 1 in *Emoll,* Nº 2 und 3 in *As dur,* Nº 4 in *Fis moll.*)

Für Clavier allein übertragen (mit untergelegtem deutschen und englischen Text) von Robert Keller

in: Brahms-Album Band II. Nº 36_39. [Pag. 4_12.] (Bd. II. compl. Pr. 5 M.)

Op. 71.
Fünf Gesänge
für eine Singstimme mit Begleitung des Pianoforte.
(Translated into English by Mrs. *Natalia Macfarren*.)
N. Simrock in Berlin. 1877.
Verlags-No 7954. [Pag. 2 _19.] Preis 4 M.

No 1. „Es liebt sich so lieblich im Lenze!" *(H. Heine.)*
"O May, love is sweet in thy bowers!"
Anmuthig bewegt.

No 2. An den Mond. *(Karl Simrock.)*
To the Moon.
Nicht zu langsam und mit Anmuth.

No 3. Geheimniss. *(Karl Candidus.)*
The secret.
Belebt und heimlich.

No 4. „Willst du, dass ich geh'?" *(Karl Lemcke.)*
"Wilt thou have me go?"
Sehr lebhaft.

№ 5. **Minnelied.** *(Hölty.)*
Lovesong.

Sehr innig, doch nicht zu langsam.

(𝑑-𝑓 oder 𝑔)   (4 Takte)   Hol-der klingt der Vo-gel-sang, wenn die
When my   ra-diant one is nigh,   when she

Die erste Ausgabe ist ohne englischen Text.
Einzeln in Ausgabe für hohe und tiefe Stimme. № 1. 2. 3. 5. Pr. à 1 M. № 4. Pr. 1 M. 50 Pf.
(In der transponirten Ausgabe (1879) steht № 1 u. 5 in *B dur*, № 2 in *G moll*, № 3 in *Es dur* u. № 4 in *C moll*.)
Für Clavier allein übertragen (mit untergelegtem deutschen und englischen Text) von ROBERT KELLER
in: Brahms-Album Band II. № 40 – 44. [Pag. 13 – 25.] (Bd. ñ. compl. Pr. 5 M.)
№ 5. (Minnelied) für Pianoforte in freier Uebertragung
(mit vorgedrucktem deutschen und englischen Text) von THEODOR KIRCHNER. 1882. Pr. 1 M. 50 Pf.
Dasselbe für Pianoforte frei bearbeitet von GUSTAV LANGE
(in: Transcriptionen beliebter Lieder von J. Brahms.) Op. 315. № 3. 1884. Pr. 1 M. 50 Pf.

Op. 72.

Fünf Gesänge

für eine Singstimme mit Begleitung des Pianoforte.

(Translated into English by Mrs. *Natalia Macfarren*.)

N. Simrock in Berlin. 1877.

Verlags-№ 7955. [Pag. 2 – 19.] Preis 4 M.

№ 1. **Alte Liebe.** *(Karl Candidus.)*
The old love.

Bewegt, doch nicht zu sehr.

(Umfang *c - 𝑓*)   Es kehrt die dun - kle Schwal - be aus
The dus - ky swal - low fly - eth to -

№ 2. **Sommerfäden.** *(Karl Candidus.)*
Gossamers.

Andante con moto.

(𝑑-𝑓)   (5 Takte)   Som - mer - fä - den hin und wie - der flie - gen von den
On the sum - mer bree - zes stray - ing gos-samer threads are

p espress.   *sempre p*

№ 3. „O kühler Wald." *(Cl. Brentano.)*
"Oh forest cool."
Langsam.

№ 4. Verzagen. *(Carl Lemcke.)*
Lament.
Bewegt. *(Con moto.)*

№ 5. Unüberwindlich. *(Goethe.)*
The untameable.
Vivace.

Die erste Ausgabe ist ohne englischen Text.
Einzeln in Ausgabe für hohe und tiefe Stimme:
№1 und 4. Pr.à 1 M.50 Pf. №2 und 3.Pr.à 80 Pf. №5. Pr.1 M.
(In der transponirten Ausgabe(1879)steht №1 und 2 in *A moll*, №3 in *B dur*, №4 in *E moll*
und №5 in *G dur*.)
Für Clavier allein übertragen (mit untergelegtem deutschen und englischen Text) von
Robert Keller in:Brahms-Album Band II.№:45_49. [Pag.26_41.]
(Bd.II.compl.Pr. 5 M.)
№1.(Alte Liebe) für Pianoforte in freier Uebertragung
(mit vorgedrucktem deutsch.u.engl.Text) von Theodor Kirchner. 1882. Pr. 1 M. 50 Pf.

8607

Op. **73.**

Zweite Symphonie (D dur)

für grosses Orchester.

N. Simrock in Berlin. 1878.

Verlags-№ 8028. Partitur [Pag. 3—71.] Preis 30 M. netto.

Orchesterstimmen (2 Fl., 2 Ob., 2 Clar., 2 Fag., 4 Hörner, 2 Tromp., 3 Posaunen, Tuba, Pauken und Streichorchester) Preis 36 M.
Einzeln: Viol. I., II., Bratsche, Violoncell und Bass Pr. à 3 M.
Für Pianoforte zu 4 Händen vom Componisten. 1878. [Pag. 2—63.] Pr. 12 M.
Für zwei Pianoforte zu 8 Händen von ROBERT KELLER. 1879. Pr. 15 M.
Für Pianoforte zu 2 Händen von ROBERT KELLER. 1880. Pr. 8 M.

Op. **74.**

Zwei Motetten

für gemischten Chor a capella.

(Translated into English by Mrs. *Natalia Macfarren*.)

Herrn *Philipp Spitta* gewidmet.

N. Simrock in Berlin. 1879.

Nº I. Verlags-Nº 8056. Partitur in 8º [Pag. 5_19.] Pr. 3 M. Nº II. Verlags-Nº 8058. Partitur in 8º [Pag. 5_15.] Pr. 2 M.

Nº 1.

„Warum ist das Licht gegeben dem Mühseligen?"

"Wherefore hath the light been giv'n to a heart sorrowful?"

Singstimmen in 8º Pr. 4 M. Einzeln (Sopran, Alt, Tenor, Bass,) Pr. à 1 M.

Nº 2.

„O Heiland, reiss' die Himmel auf"_

*"Oh Saviour, ope the heav'nly gates"*_

Singstimmen in 8º Pr. 2 M. Einzeln (Sopran, Alt, Tenor, Bass,) Pr. à 50 Pf.

Op. 75.

Balladen und Romanzen

für zwei Singstimmen mit Pianoforte.
(Translated into English by Mrs. *Natalia Macfarren*.)
Seinem Freunde *Julius Allgeyer* zugeeignet.

N. Simrock in Berlin. 1878.

N.º 1. (ALT und TENOR.)

Edward. (Schottische Ballade. Aus *Herders* Volksliedern.)

Edward.

Allegro.

Dein Schwert, wie ist's von Blut so roth?
My son, why doth thy sword drop blood?

N.º 2. (SOPRAN und ALT.)

Guter Rath. (Aus *des Knaben Wunderhorn*.)

Counsels.

Lebhaft und lustig.

Allegretto grazioso.

Ach Mut-ter, lie-be Mut-ter, ach gebt mir ei-nen
Oh Mo-ther, dear my Mo-ther, a counsel give to

N.º 3. (SOPRAN und TENOR.)

„So lass uns wandern!“ (Nach dem Böhmischen von *Joseph Wenzig*.)

"Thus we will wander!"

Anmuthig bewegt und sehr innig.

Andante grazioso e molto espressivo.

Ach Mäd-chen, lie-bes Mäd-chen, wie
Ah maid, of maids the fai--rest, thine

N.º 4. (SOPRAN I und II.)

Walpurgisnacht. (*Willibald Alexis*.)

Walpurgisnight.

Presto.

Lieb' Mut--ter, heut' Nacht heul-te Re-gen und
Good Mo--ther, last night how the tem--pest blew

Die erste Ausgabe ist ohne englischen Text.

N.º 2 und 3 für Clavier allein übertragen (mit untergelegtem deutschen und englischen Text) von ROBERT KELLER
in: Brahms-Album Band III. N.º 74. 75. [Pag. 34—41.] (Bd. III. compl. Pr. 5 M.)
N.º 3. (So lass uns wandern!) für Pianoforte in freier Uebertragung (mit vorgedrucktem deutschen und englischen Text) von THEODOR KIRCHNER. 1882. Pr. 1 M. 50 Pf.

Op. **76.**

Clavierstücke.

ZWEI HEFTE.

N. Simrock in Berlin. 1879.

Heft I. Verlags-N♀ 8090. [Pag. 3—18.] Preis 4 M.

Heft II. Verlags-N♀ 8091. [Pag. 3—18.] Preis 4 M.

HEFT I.

N♀ **1.** CAPRICCIO. Un poco agitato. *Unruhig bewegt.*

N♀ **2.** CAPRICCIO. Allegretto non troppo.

N♀ **3.** INTERMEZZO. Grazioso. *Anmuthig, ausdrucksvoll.*

N♀ **4.** INTERMEZZO. Allegretto grazioso.

HEFT II.

N♀ **5.** CAPRICCIO. Agitato, ma non troppo presto. *Sehr aufgeregt, doch nicht zu schnell.*

N♀ **6.** INTERMEZZO. Andante con moto. *Sanft bewegt.*

N♀ **7.** INTERMEZZO. Moderato semplice.

N♀ **8.** CAPRICCIO. Grazioso ed un poco vivace. *Anmuthig lebhaft.*

Op. 77.
Concert für Violine
mit Begleitung des Orchesters.
Joseph Joachim zugeeignet.
N. Simrock in Berlin. 1879.
Verlags-№ 8133. Partitur in 8º | Pag. 5_208. | Pr. 20 M. netto.

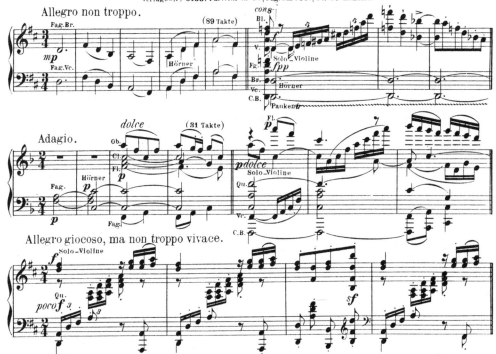

Orchesterstimmen (2 Fl., 2 Ob., 2 Cl., 2 Fag., 4 Hörner, 2 Tromp., Pauken und Streichorchester)
ohne Principalstimme. Pr. 18 M.
Einzeln: Viol. I., II., Bratsche Pr. à 1 M. 50 Pf. Violoncell und Contrabass Pr. 2 M. 50 Pf.
Principalstimme. [Pag. 1 _ 17.] Pr. 3 M.
Ausgabe mit Clavierbegleitung. 1879. [Pag. 3 _ 39.] Pr. 10 M.
Für Pianoforte zu vier Händen bearbeitet von ROBERT KELLER. 1880. Pr. 9 M.

Op. 78.
Sonate
für Pianoforte und Violine.
N. Simrock in Berlin. 1880.
Verlags-№ 8148. Partitur [Pag. 3 _ 31] und Stimme. Preis 7 M. 50 Pf.

Für Pianoforte zu 4 Händen bearbeitet von ROBERT KELLER. 1880. Pr. 6 M.

Op. **79.**

Zwei Rhapsodien

für das Pianoforte.

Frau *Elisabeth von Herzogenberg* gewidmet.

N. Simrock in Berlin. 1880.

Verlags-N9 8166. [Pag. 2_19.] Preis 4 M.

№ 1.

Agitato.

№ 2.

Molto passionato, ma non troppo allegro.

Op. **80.**

Akademische Fest-Ouverture

für grosses Orchester.

N. Simrock in Berlin. 1881.

Verlags-N9 8187. Partitur in 89 [Pag. 5_71.] Pr. 12 M. netto.

Allegro.

SCHLUSSSATZ. *(Gaudeamus igitur)*

Maestoso.

Orchesterstimmen (Piccolo, 2 Fl., 2 Ob., 2 Cl., 2 Fag., Contrafag.. 4 Hörner, 3 Tromp.,
3 Posaunen, Tuba, Pauken, Gr.Trommel mit Becken, Triangel und Streichorchester) Pr. 16 M.
Einzeln: Viol.I., II., Bratsche Pr. à 1 M. Vell. u. C.Bass Pr. 2 M.
Für Pianoforte zu 4 Händen vom Componisten. [Pag. 2_27.] 1881. Pr. 6 M.
Für 2 Pianoforte zu 8 Händen von ROBERT KELLER. 1882. Pr. 8 M.
Für Pianoforte zu 2 Händen von ROBERT KELLER. 1882. Pr. 3 M.

Op. 81.
Tragische Ouverture
für Orchester.
N. Simrock in Berlin. 1881.
Verlags-No 8189. Partitur in 8º [Pag. 5—71.] Pr. 12 M. netto.

Allegro ma non troppo.

Orchesterstimmen (Piccolo, 2 Fl., 2 Ob., 2 Clar., 2 Fag., 4 Hörner,
2 Tromp., 3 Posaunen, Tuba, Pauken und Streichorchester) Preis 16 M.
Einzeln: Viol. I., II., Bratsche Pr.à 1 M. Vcll. u. C.Bass Pr. 2 M.
Für Pianoforte zu 4 Händen vom Componisten. 1881. [Pag. 2—27.] Pr. 6 M.
Für 2 Pianoforte zu 8 Händen von Robert Keller. 1882. Pr. 8 M.
Für Pianoforte zu 2 Händen von Robert Keller. 1882. Pr 3 M.

Op. 82.
Nänie
von *Friedrich Schiller*
für Chor und Orchester (Harfe ad libitum.)
Frau Hofrath *Henriette Feuerbach* zugeeignet.
(Englische Uebersetzung von Mrs. *J. P. Morgan*.)
Leipzig, C.F. Peters. 1881.
Verlags-No 6525. Edition Peters No 2081. Partitur [Pag. 3—29.] Pr. 6 M. netto.

Andante. (♩ = 100.)

In die Edition Peters (No 2081) aufgenommen.
Orchesterstimmen (2 Fl., 2 Ob., 2 Clar., 2 Fag., 2 Hörner, 3 Posaunen, Pauken, Harfe
und Streichorchester) Preis 7 M. 80 Pf. netto.
Einzeln: Viol. I., II., Viola, Violoncell, Contrabass, Preis jeder Stimme 60 Pf.
Chorstimmen in 8º Pr. 3 M. Einzeln: Sopran, Alt, Tenor, Bass, Pr. à 75 Pf.
Clavierauszug mit Text Pr. 3 M.

Op. 83.

(Zweites) Concert (*B dur*)

für Pianoforte mit Begleitung des Orchesters.

Seinem theuren Freunde und Lehrer *Eduard Marxsen* zugeeignet.

N. Simrock in Berlin. 1882.

Verlags-No 8263. Partitur [Pag. 3 — 159.] Preis 30 M.n.

Orchesterstimmen (2 Fl., 2 Ob., 2 Clar., 2 Fag., 4 Hörner,
2 Tromp., Pauken und Streichorchester) Preis 25 M.
Einzeln: Viol. I., II., Bratsche Pr. à 2 M. Vcell.und C.Bass Pr. 4 M.
Ausgabe für Piano solo. [Pag. 3 — 60.] 1882. Pr. 10 M.
Für zwei Pianoforte vom Componisten. (In Partitur gestochen, so dass zur Ausführung
zwei Exemplare nöthig sind.) [Pag. 3 — 110.] 1882. Pr. 20 M.
Für Pianoforte zu 4 Händen bearbeitet von ROBERT KELLER. 1882. Pr. 15 M.

Op. 84.
Romanzen und Lieder
für eine oder zwei Stimmen
mit Begleitung des Pianoforte.
(Translated into English by Mrs. *Natalia Macfarren.*)
N. Simrock in Berlin. 1882.
Verlags-№ 8298. [Pag. 3—23] Preis 4 M.

N.° 1. Sommerabend. *(Hans Schmidt.)*
Summer evening.
Andante con moto.
(DIE MUTTER.) *(THE MOTHER.)*

Geh schla- -fen, Toch- ter, schla- - -fen! Schon fällt der
Go slum- -ber, daugh- ter, slum- - -ber! With dew the

N.° 2. Der Kranz. *(Hans Schmidt.)*
The wreath.
Allegro grazioso. (Lebhaft.)   (DIE TOCHTER.) *(THE DAUGHTER.)*

Mut- ter, hilf mir ar- men Toch- ter,
Mo- ther, hear thy troubled daugh- ter,

p leggiero

N.° 3. In den Beeren. *(Hans Schmidt.)*
Amongst the berries.
Sehr lebhaft.   (DIE MUTTER.) *(THE MOTHER.)*

(4 Takte)

Sin- ge, Mäd- chen, hell und klar, sing' aus
Sing, my daugh- ter, clear and loud, strain that

N.° 4. Vergebliches Ständchen. *(Niederrheinisches Volkslied.)*
The vain suit.
Lebhaft und gut gelaunt.   (ER.) *(HE.)*

Gu- ten A- bend, mein Schatz, gu- ten A- bend, mein Kind,
Fair good- e- ven, my dar- ling, good- e- ven, my dear,

N⁰ 5. Spannung. (Niederrheinisches Volkslied.)
Strained greetings.

Bewegt und heimlich.

(ER.) (HE.)

Für Clavier allein übertragen
(mit untergelegtem deutschen und englischen Text) von ROBERT KELLER in:
Brahms-Album Band III. N⁰ 76–80. [Pag. 42–58.] (Bd. III. compl. Pr. 5 M.)
N⁰ 4. (Vergebliches Ständchen) für Pianoforte frei bearbeitet von GUSTAV LANGE
(in „Transcriptionen beliebter Lieder von J. Brahms") Op. 315. N⁰ 1. 1884. Pr. 1 M. 50 Pf.
Dasselbe (N⁰ 4 einzeln) in Ausgabe für hohe, mittlere (G dur) und tiefe
Stimme (F dur). 1886. Preis à 2 M.
Dasselbe für 4 st. Männerchor a capella bearb. v. ROBERT FUCHS. Partitur Pr. 2 M. Stimmen Pr. 2 M., einzeln à 50 Pf.

Op. 85.

Sechs Lieder
für eine Stimme mit Begleitung des Pianoforte.
(Translated into English by Mrs. *Natalia Macfarren*.)
N. Simrock in Berlin. 1882.
Verlags-N⁰ 8299. [Pag. 3–19.] Preis 4 M.

N⁰ 1. Sommerabend. (*H. Heine.*)
Summer eve.

Langsam.

N⁰ 2. Mondenschein. (*H. Heine.*)
Moonbeams.

Langsam.

No 3. Mädchenlied. *(Siegfried Kapper. Serbisch.)*
Servian maiden's song.

No 4. Ade! *(Siegfried Kapper. Nach dem Böhmischen.)*
Farewell.

No 5. Frühlingslied. *(Emanuel Geibel.)*
Spring morn.

No 6. In Waldeseinsamkeit. *(Karl Lemcke.)*
In lonely wood.

Transponirte Ausgabe für eine tiefere Stimme. 1882. Pr. 4 M.
(No 1. 2 u. 6 stehen in *G dur*, No 3 in *F moll*, No 4 in *G moll* und No 5 in *E dur*.)
Für Clavier allein übertragen (mit untergelegtem deutschen und englischen Text) von
Robert Keller in: Brahms-Album. Band II. No 50_55. [Pag. 42 _ 53.] (Bd.II. compl. Pr. 5 M.)

8607

Op. 86.
Sechs Lieder
für eine tiefere Stimme mit Begleitung des Pianoforte.
(Translated into English by Mrs. *Natalia Macfarren*.)
N. Simrock in Berlin. 1882.
Verlags-No 8300. [Pag. 4 — 21.] Preis 4 M.

Nº 1. Therese. *(Gottfried Keller.)*
Teresa.

Nº 2. Feldeinsamkeit. *(Hermann Allmers.)*
In summer fields.

Nº 3. Nachtwandler. *(Max Kalbeck.)*
The sleeper.

Nº 4. Ueber die Haide. *(Theodor Storm.)*
Over the moor.

Nº 5. Versunken. *(Felix Schumann.)*
Engulphed.
Sehr leidenschaftlich, doch nicht zu rasch.

Es brau-sen der Lie-be Wo — gen und
The bil_lows of love are brea-king, and

Nº 6. Todessehnen. *(Max von Schenkendorf.)*
Shadows of death.
Langsam.

Ach, wer nimmt von mei — ner See-le die ge — hei-me, schwe-re Last,
Ah, when shall I cast the bur_den that weighs down my spi — rit's wings,

Transponirte Ausgabe fur hohe Stimme. 1882. Pr. 4 M.
(Nº 1 steht in *F dur*, Nº 2 u. 5 in *A dur*, Nº 3 in *D dur*, Nº 4 u. 6 in *A moll*.)
Für Clavier allein übertragen (mit untergelegtem deutschen und englischen Text) von ROBERT KELLER
in: Brahms-Album Band II. Nº 56 — 61. [Pag. 54 — 70.] (Bd. II. compl. Pr. 5 M.)

Op. 87.
Trio
für Pianoforte, Violine und Violoncell.
N. Simrock in Berlin. 1883.
Verlags-Nº 8324. Partitur [Pag. 3 — 67] und Stimmen Preis 12 M.

(THEMA MIT VARIATIONEN.)
Andante con moto.

Allegro. (♩ = 138.)

SCHERZO.
Presto.

FINALE.
Allegro giocoso.

Für Pianoforte zu 4 Händen von ROBERT KELLER. 1883. Pr. 10 M.

Op. 88.

Quintett

für zwei Violinen, zwei Bratschen und Violoncell.

N. Simrock in Berlin. 1883.

Verlags–N⁰ 8314. Partitur in 8⁰ [Pag. 3—51] Pr. 6 M. netto.

I.

Allegro non troppo ma con brio.

II. Grave ed appassionato.

Allegretto vivace.

Tempo I⁰.

Presto.

III. (FINALE.)

Tempo I⁰. Allegro energico.

Stimmen Preis 10 M.
Für Pianoforte zu 4 Händen vom Componisten. [Pag. 2— 43] 1883. Pr. 8 M.

Op. 89.

Gesang der Parzen

von Goethe

(Song of the Fates.)

(Translated into English by Mrs. *Natalia Macfarren.*)

für sechsstimmigen Chor und Orchester.

Seiner Hoheit dem Herzog *Georg von Sachsen-Meiningen* ehrerbietigst zugeeignet.

N. Simrock in Berlin. 1883.

Verlags–N⁰ 8317. Partitur [Pag. 6—31] Pr. 7 M. 50 Pf. netto.

Maestoso.

Es fürch - te die Göt - ter das
In fear of the Gods shall ye

Menschen-geschlecht! Es fürch-te die Göt-ter das Menschen-geschlecht! Sie hal-ten die
dwell, sons of men! In fear of the Gods shall ye dwell, sons of men! Sole em-pire they

Die erste Ausgabe ist ohne englischen Text.

Orchesterstimmen (2 Fl., 2 Ob., 2 Clar., 2 Fag., Contrafag., 4 Hörner, 2 Tromp., 3 Pos.,
(kl. Fl.) Tuba, Pauken und Streichorchester) Pr. 12 M.

Einzeln: Violine I., II., Bratsche, Violoncell, Contrabass Pr. à 80 Pf.

Chorstimmen in 8° Pr. 4 M. 80 Pf.

Einzeln: Sopran, Alt I., II., Tenor, Bass I., II. Pr. à 80 Pf.

Clavierauszug mit Text in 8° [Pag. 5—26] 1883. Pr. 3 M. netto.

Für Pianoforte zu 2 Händen (mit untergelegtem deutsch. u. engl. Text) von ROBERT KELLER. 1883. Pr. 3 M.

Für Pianoforte zu 4 Händen „ „ „ „ „ von ROBERT KELLER. 1883. Pr. 3 M.

Op. 90.
Dritte Symphonie *(F dur)*
für grosses Orchester.
N. Simrock in Berlin. 1884.
Verlags-N° 8454. Partitur [Pag. 5—109] Preis 30 M. netto.

Orchesterstimmen (2 Fl., 2 Ob., 2 Clar., 2 Fag., Contrafag., 4 Hörner, 2 Tromp., 3 Pos.,
Pauken und Streichorchester) Pr. 36 M.

Einzeln: Viol. I., II., Bratsche Pr. à 3 M. Violoncell Pr. 2 M. 50 Pf. Contrabass Pr. 2 M.

Für zwei Pianoforte (zu 4 Händen) vom Componisten. Partitur-Ausgabe. [Pag. 3—62] 1884. Pr. 12 M.
Zweites Clavier apart. Pr. 6 M.

Für zwei Pianoforte zu 8 Händen von ROBERT KELLER. 1884. Pr. 15 M.

Für Pianoforte zu 2 Händen von ROBERT KELLER. 1884. Pr. 8 M.

Für Pianoforte zu 4 Händen von ROBERT KELLER. (Satz I u. III überarbeitet vom Componisten.) Pr. 12 M.

Op. 91.

Zwei Gesänge

für eine Altstimme mit Bratsche und Pianoforte.

(English words by Mrs. *John P. Morgan* of New-York.)

N. Simrock in Berlin. 1884.

Verlags-No 8474. Partitur [Pag. 3—19] und Stimmen Pr. 4 M. 50 Pf.

No 1. Gestillte Sehnsucht. *(Friedrich Rückert.)*

Longing at rest.

Adagio espressivo.

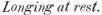

In goldnen A-bend-schein ge-tauchet, wie
In evenings gol-den twi- -light wreathed, how

No 2. Geistliches Wiegenlied. (Nach *Lope de Vega* von *Emanuel Geibel.*)

Cradle song of the Virgin.

Andante con moto.

Die ihr schwebet um diese Pal-men,
Ye who o'er these palms are hov'-ring;

(Jo-sef, lie-ber Jo-sef mein,)
(Joseph, dearest Joseph mine,)

★ Altes Lied.
Ancient Song.

Op. 92.

Quartette

für Sopran, Alt, Tenor und Bass mit Pianoforte.

(English version by Mrs. *John P. Morgan* of New-York.)

N. Simrock in Berlin. 1884.

Verlags-No 8477. Partitur [Pag. 3—22.] Preis 5 M.

No 1. O schöne Nacht! *(G. Fr. Daumer.)*

O charming night!

Andante con moto.

O schö - - -
O charm - - -

№ 2. Spätherbst. *(Hermann Allmers.)*
Late Autumn.

№ 3. Abendlied. *(Friedrich Hebbel.)*
Even-Song.

№ 4. Warum? *(Goethe.)*
Why?

Stimmen in 8º (Sopran, Alt, Tenor, Bass) Pr. 4 M. Einzeln à 1 M.

Lieder und Romanzen
für vierstimmigen gemischten Chor (a capella)
(English version by Mrs. *John P. Morgan* of New-York.)
N. Simrock in Berlin. 1884.
Verlags-No 8479. Partitur in 8º [Pag. 3—27] Preis 4 M.

Nº 1. Der bucklichte Fiedler. (Rheinisches Volkslied.)
The hump-backed fiddler.

Nº 2. Das Mädchen. (Serbisch. *Siegfr. Kapper.*)
The maiden.

Zu Nº 2 vgl. Op. 95 Nº 1.

Nº 3. „O süsser Mai!" (*L. Achim von Arnim.*)
"O lovely May."

Nº 4. Fahr' wohl! (*Friedrich Rückert.*)
Fare well.

Nº 5. Der Falke. (Serbisch. *Siegfried Kapper.*)
The falcon.

Nº 6. Beherzigung. (*Goethe.*)
Stout hearted.

Stimmen in 8º Pr. 4 M. Einzeln: (Sopran, Alt, Tenor, Bass) jede Stimme Pr. 1 M.

Op. **93** ♭

Tafellied
(Dank der Damen)
von Joseph von Eichendorff
(*"Drinking Glee"*)
(English version by Mrs. *John P. Morgan* of New-York.)
für sechsstimmigen gemischten Chor mit Pianoforte.
Den *Freunden in Crefeld* zum 28sten Jan. 1885.
N. Simrock in Berlin. 1885.

Chorstimmen (Sopran, Alt I., II., Tenor, Bass I., II., Pr. à 50 Pf.) in 8º Pr. 3 M.

Op. **94**.

Fünf Lieder
für eine tiefe Stimme mit Begleitung des Pianoforte.
(English words by Mrs. *John P. Morgan* of New-York.)
N. Simrock in Berlin. 1884.

Nº **1**. Mit vierzig Jahren. *(Friedrich Rückert.)*
At forty.
Langsam.

№ 2. „Steig' auf, geliebter Schatten" *(Friedrich Halm.)*
"Arise, beloved spirit."
Gehalten.

Steig auf, ge-liebter Schat-ten, vor mir in tod-ter
A - rise, be-lo-ved spir - it, to me in dead of

№ 3. „Mein Herz ist schwer" *(Emanuel Geibel.)*
"My heart is sad."
Unruhig bewegt, doch nicht schnell.

Mein Herz_ ist schwer, mein Au - ge wacht, der
My heart_ is sad, mine eyes_ a-light, the

№ 4. Sapphische Ode. *(Hans Schmidt.)*
Sapphic Ode.
Ziemlich langsam.

Ro-sen brach ich Nachts mir am dunklen Ha - ge;
Ro - ses ga-thered I in the night by dark-ling way;

№ 5. „Kein Haus, keine Heimath" *(aus einem Drama v. Friedrich Halm.)*
"No home, no country."
Tempo giusto.

Kein Haus, kei-ne Hei-math, kein Weib und kein
No home, and no coun-try, no wife, and no

Ausgabe für hohe Stimme. 1884. Pr. 4 M.
(№ 1 steht in *D moll*, № 2 in *F moll*, № 3 in *B moll*, № 4 in *F dur* und № 5 in *Fis moll*.)

Op. 95.

Sieben Lieder

für eine Singstimme mit Begleitung des Pianoforte.

English words by Mrs. *John P. Morgan* of New-York.

N. Simrock in Berlin. 1884.

Verlags-No 8489. [Pag. 3—23.] Preis 4 M.

Nº 1.

Das Mädchen. (Serbisch. *Siegfried Kapper.*)

A maiden.

Munter, mit freiem Vortrag.

(Umfang) Stand das Mädchen, stand am Berges-ab-hang, wiederschien der Berg von ih-rem Ant-litz,
(e-gis) *Stood a maiden, stood on mountain fastness, saw her i-mage on the mount re-flected,*

mf

Zu Nº 1 vgl. Op. 93ª Nº 2.

Nº 2.

„Bei dir sind meine Gedanken" (*Friedrich Halm.*)

"With thee my thoughts are forever"

Schnell und heimlich.

(e-fis) (5 Takte) Bei dir sind mei-ne Ge-dan-ken
With thee my thoughts are for-ev-er

p sotto voce

Nº 3.

Beim Abschied. (*Friedrich Halm.*)

Parting.

Sehr lebhaft und ungeduldig.

(fis-fis) (5 Takte) Ich müh' mich ab, und kann's nicht verschmer-zen, und
I try my best, but all un-a-vail-ing, the

f *p*

Nº 4.
Der Jäger. (*Friedrich Halm.*)
The huntsman.

Lebhaft.

Mein Lieb ist ein Jä — — ger, und grün ist sein
My love is a hun — — ter, coat green as you

Nº 5.
Vorschneller Schwur. (Serbisch. *Siegfried Kapper.*)
A hasty oath.

Allegretto.
(*Angemessen frei vorzutragen*)

Schwor ein jun — ges Mäd — chen: Blu — men nie zu tra — gen,
Swore a young, a young maid-en, flowers nev-er, ne'er to wear,

Nº 6.
Mädchenlied. (*Paul Heyse.* Nach dem Italienischen.)
Maiden Song.

Behaglich.

Am jüngsten Tag ich auf-er-steh, und gleich nach mei — nem Lieb-sten seh,
At the last day when rise I may, and quickly look my sweet-heart's way,

Nº 7.
„Schön war, das ich dir weihte"— (*G. F. Daumer.*)
"Fine was, the gift I gave thee"

Einfach.

Schön war, das ich dir weih-te, das gol-de-ne Geschmei — de;
Fine was, the gift I gave thee, the shining gold-en jewels rare;

Ausgabe für tiefe Stimme.1884.Pr.4 M.
(Nº 1 steht in *G moll*, Nº 2 in *F dur*, Nº 3 in *B dur*, Nº 4 in *D dur*, Nº 5 in *B moll*,
Nº 6 in *Des dur* und Nº 7 in *D moll*.)

Op. 96.
Vier Lieder
für eine Singstimme mit Begleitung des Pianoforte.
(Aeusserer und innerer Titel nach Originalzeichnungen von *M. Klinger.*)
(English text by Mrs. *John P. Morgan* of New-York.)
N. Simrock in Berlin. 1886.
Verlags-№ 8626. [Pag. 4—15.] Preis 4 M.

№ 1. „Der Tod, das ist die kühle Nacht." (*H. Heine.*)
"*Death is the cooling Night*"

Ausgabe für tiefere Stimme 1886. Pr. 4 M.
(№ 1 steht in *As dur,* № 2 in *B dur,* № 3 in *G moll* und № 4 in *F moll.*)
8607

Op. 97.

Sechs Lieder

für eine Singstimme mit Begleitung des Pianoforte.

(Aeusserer und innerer Titel nach Originalzeichnungen von *M. Klinger*.)

(English text by Mrs. *John P. Morgan* of New-York.)

N. Simrock in Berlin. 1886.

Verlags- No 8627. [Pag. 3 – 19.] Preis 4 M.

No 1.

Nachtigall. (*C. Reinhold*.)

Nightingale.

No 2.

Auf dem Schiffe. (*C. Reinhold*.)

"A birdling flew"—

No 3.

Entführung. (*Willibald Alexis*.)

"O Lady Judith"—

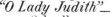

No 4.

„Dort in den Weiden"— (Niederrheinisches Volkslied.)

"There 'mong the willows"—

102

№ 5.

Komm bald. *(Klaus Groth.)*

Come soon.

Zart bewegt.

№ 6.

Trennung. *(Schwäbisch.)*

The Parting. (Swabian.)

Anmuthig bewegt.

(*dis-g*) (4 Takte) Wa-rum denn war-ten
Waiting, why art thou

(*e-f*) (4 Takte) Da un - ten im Tha - le läuft's
Down there in the val - ley the

Ausgabe für tiefere Stimme. 1886. Pr. 4 M.

(In der transponirten Ausgabe steht № 1 in *D moll,* № 2 in *F dur,* № 3 in *C moll,*
№ 4 in *B dur,* № 5 in *G dur,* № 6 in *Es dur.*)

№ 4. (Dort in den Weiden) für vierstimmigen Männerchor *a capella* bearbeitet von ROBERT FUCHS.
Partitur. Preis **2 M.** Stimmen: Pr. **2 M.** Einzeln: Tenor I., II., Bass I., II. Pr. à **50 Pf.**

№ 6. (Trennung) für vierstimmigen Männerchor *a capella* bearbeitet von ROBERT FUCHS.
Partitur. Preis **2 M.** Stimmen: Pr. **2 M.** Einzeln: Tenor I., II., Bass I., II. Pr. à **50 Pf.**

Op. 98.

Vierte Symphonie *(E moll)*

für grosses Orchester.

N. Simrock in Berlin. 1886.

Verlags-№ 8686. Partitur [Pag. 4 — 113.] Preis 30 M. netto.

Allegro non troppo.

8607

Allegro energico e passionato.
TEMA con VARIAZIONI.)

(VAR.I.)

Orchesterstimmen (Piccolo, 2 Fl., 2 Ob., 2 Cl., 2 Fag., Contrafag., 4 Hörner, 2 Tromp., 3 Pos.,
Pauken, Triangel und Streichorchester) Preis 36 M.

Einzeln: Viol.I., II., Bratsche, Violoncell, Contrabass. Preis à 3 M.

Für zwei Pianoforte (zu 4 Händen) vom COMPONISTEN. Partitur-Ausgabe.[Pag. 2–83.]1886.Pr.16 M.
Zweites Clavier apart. Preis 8 M.

Für zwei Pianoforte zu 8 Händen von ROBERT KELLER.1886.Preis 15 M.

Für Pianoforte zu 2 Händen von ROBERT KELLER.1886. Preis 8 M.

Für Pianoforte zu 4 Händen vom COMPONISTEN. 1886. Preis 12 M.

Op.99.
Sonate
für Violoncell und Pianoforte.
N.Simrock in Berlin. 1887.
Verlags-N? 8750. [Pag. 3 – 30.] Preis 8 M.

Allegro vivace.

Adagio affettuoso.   **Allegro passionato.**

Allegro molto.

Op. **100.**
Sonate
für Violine und Pianoforte.

N. Simrock in Berlin. 1887.

Verlags-№ 8751. [Pag. 3 _27.] Preis **8** M.

I. Allegro amabile.

II. Andante tranquillo.

Vivace (alternativo.)

III. Allegretto grazioso (quasi Andante).

Op. **101.**
Trio
für Pianoforte, Violine und Violoncell.

N. Simrock in Berlin. 1887.

Verlags-№ 8752. [Pag. 2 _35.] Partitur und Stimmen. Pr. **12** M.

Allegro energico.

Presto non assai.

Andante grazioso.

Allegro molto.

Op. 102.
Concert
für Violine und Violoncell
mit Begleitung des Orchesters.

N. Simrock in Berlin. 1888.

Verlags-N? 8964. Partitur in 4? [Pag. 3-130] Pr. 30 M. netto.

Allegro.

Vivace non troppo.

Orchesterstimmen (2 Fl., 2 Ob., 2 Cl., 2 Fag., 4 Hörner, 2 Tromp., Pauken und Streichorchester) ohne Principal Stimmen. Pr. 24 M.
Einzeln: Viol. I. II, Bratsche, Violoncell, Contrabass, Pr. à 1 M. 50 Pf.
Principal Stimmen [Pag. 1-23] Pr. à 4 M.
Ausgabe mit Clavierbegleitung. 1888. [Pag. 3-47] Pr. 15 M.
Für Pianoforte zu vier Händen bearbeitet von Robert Keller. 1889. Pr. 10 M.

Op. 103.

Zigeunerlieder.

Gipsy Songs.

Für vier Singstimmen (Sopran, Alt, Tenor und Bass)
mit Begleitung des Pianoforte.
Nach dem Ungarischen von *Hugo Conrat.*
(English Text by Mrs. *John P. Morgan* of New-York.)
N. Simrock in Berlin. 1888.

Verlags-No 9026. Partitur [Pag. 3-30] Pr. 4 M. 50 Pf. netto.

Singstimmen in 8º Text deutsch und englisch. Pr. 6 M. Einzeln (S.A.T.B.) Pr. à 1 M. 50 Pf.
Für Pianoforte zu vier Händen von THEODOR KIRCHNER. 1888. Pr. 5 M.
Für Pianoforte solo von THEODOR KIRCHNER. 1888. Pr. 4 M.
Acht Zigeunerlieder (Nº 1.2.3.4.5.6.7.11 der Original Partitur) für eine Singstimme mit Begleitung des Pianoforte bearbeitet vom COMPONISTEN. 1889. Text deutsch und englisch. Pr. 4 M.
Themata siehe oben angeführte Nummern der Partitur. (Nº 7 steht hier in *E dur*).
Ausgabe für tiefe Stimme. 1889. Pr. 4 M.
(Nº 1 steht in *F moll*, Nº 2 in *B moll*, Nº 3 in *B dur*, Nº 4 in *D dur*, Nº 5 in *H dur*, Nº 6 in *Es dur*, Nº 7 in *C dur* und Nº 8 in *B dur*.)
Zigeunerlied (aus Op.103. Nº 7.) für Pianoforte übertragen von ILDA TILIKE. 1896. Pr. 80 Pf.

Op. 104.

Fünf Gesänge

für gemischten Chor (a Capella).

(English version by Mrs. *John P. Morgan* of New-York.)

N. Simrock in Berlin. 1889.

Verlags-№ 9053. Partitur in 8º [Pag. 4-26] Pr. 4 M.

№ 1. Nachtwache.(I.) *(Fr. Rückert.)*

Nightwatch. (I.)

Langsam.

Slowly.

№ 2. Nachtwache. (II.) *(Fr. Rückert.)*

Nightwatch. (II.)

Feierlich bewegt.

Solemnly.

№ 3. Letztes Glück. *(Max Kalbeck.)*

Last happiness.

Ziemlich langsam.

Rather slowly.

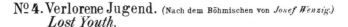

№ 4. Verlorene Jugend. (Nach dem Böhmischen von *Josef Wenzig.*)

Lost Youth.

Lebhaft, doch nicht zu schnell.

Spirited, but not too fast.

№ 5. Im Herbst. *(Klaus Groth.)*

In Autumn.

Andante.

Stimmen in 8º. Text deutsch und englisch. Pr. 4 M.   Einzeln (S.A.T.B.) Pr. à 1 M.

Op. 105.

Fünf Lieder

für eine tiefere Stimme mit Begleitung des Pianoforte.

(English Text by Mrs. *John P. Morgan* of New-York.)

N. Simrock in Berlin. 1889.

Verlags-Nº 9042. [Pag. 4–21] Pr. 4 M.

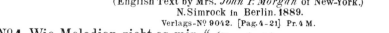

Nº 1. „Wie Melodien zieht es mir—" *(Klaus Groth.)*

"Like Melodies—"

Zart.

Tenderly.

(Umfang)
a–e

Wie Me - lo - di - en zieht es mir lei - se durch den
Like me - lo - dies it flow - eth, soft thro' my spir - it

p sempre dolce

Nº 2. „Immer leiser wird mein Schlummer—" *(Hermann Lingg.)*

"Faint and fainter is my slumber—"

Langsam und leise.

Slow and soft.

(*a–f*)

Im - mer lei - ser wird mein Schlum - mer, nur wie
Faint and faint - er is my slum - ber, But a

pp sempre e legato

Nº 3. Klage. *(Vom Niederrhein.)*

Plaint. (Lower-Rhinelandish.)

Einfach und ausdrucksvoll.

Simply and with expression.

1. Fein's Liebchen, trau du nicht, dass er dein Herz nicht bricht! Schön' Wor - te will er
1. *Fair love, trust not his art, That he may break thy heart! Sweet words with him are*
(*d–d*) (3 Verse)

Andante espressivo.

p dol.

Nº 4. Auf dem Kirchhofe. *(Detlev von Liliencron.)*

In the Church Yard.

Mässig.

Moderato.

Der Tag ging re - genschwer und
The day pass'd dark with rain and
(*h–es*)

Andante moderato.

f
3 Takte
mf

8607

N⁰ 5. Verrath. *(Carl Lemcke.)*
Treachery.
Angemessen bewegt.
Tempo appropriate.

Ich stand in ei - ner lau - en Nacht an
I stood, up-on a sum-mernight,There

Con moto. *(fis-dis)*

Transponirte Ausgabe für hohe Stimme. 1889. Pr. 4 M.
(N⁰1 steht in *Cdur*, N⁰2 in *Fmoll*, N⁰3 in *Gmoll*, N⁰4 in *Emoll* und N⁰5 in *Es moll*.)
N⁰1.„Wie Melodien zieht es mir-" für Violoncell und Pianoforte in: Album für Violoncell
von NORBERT SALTER (Pr. 2 M.40 Pf. netto.)

Op. 106.
Fünf Lieder
für eine Singstimme mit Begleitung des Pianoforte.
(English Text by Mrs. *John P. Morgan* of New-York.)
N. Simrock in Berlin. 1889.
Verlags-N⁰ 9043. [Pag. 3-19] Pr. 4 M.

N⁰ 1. Ständchen. *(Franz Kugler.)*
The Serenade.
Anmuthig bewegt.
Moring gracefully.

Allegretto grazioso.
(3 Takte)

(Umfang)
d - g

Der Mond steht ü-berdem Ber - ge, so recht für ver-
The moon hangs ov-er the mountain, just right for

N⁰ 2. Auf dem See. *(C. Reinhold.)*
On the sea.
Anmuthig bewegt und ausdrucksvoll.
Gracefully and with expression.

(dis-gis)
p grazioso

An dies Schiff-lein schmie - ge, hol - der See, dich
To this shal - lop lock thee, Gen - tle sea, so

(4 Takte)

N⁰ 3. „Es hing der Reif-" *(Klaus Groth.)*
"A Hoar-Frost hung on Lindentree-"
Träumerisch.
Dreamingly.

(d - a)

Es hing der Reif im
A hoar - - frost hung on

molto p e dolce

(3 Takte)

col 𝄢. 8607

Nº 4. Meine Lieder. *(Adolf Frey.)*
My Songs.
Bewegt und leise.
Spirited and soft.

Wenn mein Herz be - ginnt ___ zu
When my heart be - gins ___ its

Nº 5. Ein Wanderer. *(C. Reinhold.)*
A Wanderer.
In langsam gehender Bewegung.
In the movement of a slow step.

Hier, wo sich die Stra - ssen schei - den, wo nun gehn die
Here, where these two by - ways sev - er, With - er lead the

Transponirte Ausgabe für tiefe Stimme. 1889. Pr. 4 M.
(Nº 1 steht in *Es dur*, Nº 2 in *C dur*, Nº 3 in *F moll*, Nº 4 in *Dis moll* und Nº 5 in *D moll*.)
Nº 1. Ständchen in: Brahms, Ausgewählte Lieder. Band VII. Pr. 3 M. netto.

Op. **107.**

Fünf Lieder
für eine Singstimme mit Begleitung des Pianoforte.
(English Text by Mrs. *John P. Morgan* of New-York.)
N. Simrock in Berlin. 1889.
Verlags-Nº 9064. [Pag. 3-15] Pr. 4 M.

Nº 1. An die Stolze. *(Paul Flemming.)*
To the Proudone.
Sehr lebhaft und ausdrucksvoll.
Very spirited and with great expression.

Und gleichwohl kann ich anders nicht, ich muss ihr gün - stig sein,
And though full well I see a - right, To her must grac - ious be,

Nº 2. Salamander. *(Carl Lemcke.)*
Mit Laune.
With humor.

Es sass ein Sa - la - man - der auf ei - nem küh - len Stein, da
There sat a sal - a - man - der up - on a cold, cold stone, Him

Transponirte Ausgabe für tiefe Stimme. 1889. Pr. 4 M.
(№ 1 steht in *F dur*, № 2 in *Fis moll*, № 3 in *Fis dur*, № 4 in *C dur* und № 5 in *G moll*.)

Op. 108.

Dritte Sonate

für Violine und Pianoforte.
Seinem Freunde *Hans von Bülow* gewidmet
N. Simrock in Berlin. 1889.
Verlags-№ 9196. [Pag. 3-34] Pr. 8 M.

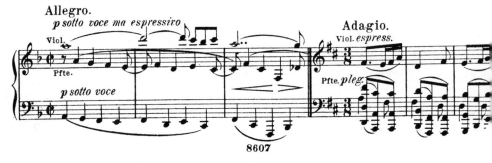

Un poco presto e con sentimento.

Presto agitato.

Für Pianoforte zu **4 Händen** bearbeitet von ROBERT KELLER. 1889. Pr. 6 M.
Adagio für Orgel arrangirt von EDWIN H. LEMARE. 1897. Pr. 1 M. 50 Pf.

Op. **109.**

Fest- und Gedenksprüche

für achtstimmigen Chor (a Capella).
(English Text adepted by Mrs. *John P. Morgan* of New-York.)
Seiner Magnificenz dem Herrn Bürgermeister *Dr. Carl Petersen*
in *Hamburg* verehrungsvoll zugeeignet.
N. Simrock in Berlin. 1890.
Verlags-N♀ **9291.** Partitur* in 8♀ [Pag. 4–50] Pr. 4 M. netto.

№ **1.**
Feierlich bewegt.
Majestic and with spirit.

№ **2.**
Lebhaft und entschlossen.
With life and decision.

№ **3.**
Froh bewegt.
Joyfully.

Singstimmen in 8♀ Text deutsch und englisch. Pr. 4 M.
Einzeln (Chor I und II auf eine Stimme gedruckt.) Pr. à 1 M.

* im Sopran-, Alt-, Tenor- und Bass-Schlüssel (mit untergelegtem Klavierauszuge, nur zur etwaigen Aushülfe beim Einstudiren).

114

Op. 110.

Drei Motetten

für vier- und achtstimmigen Chor (a Capella).

(English Text adepted by Mrs. *John P. Morgan* of New-York.)

N. Simrock in Berlin. 1890.

Verlags-Nº 9306. Partitur* in 8º [Pag. 3-84] Pr. 3 M. netto.

Singstimmen in 8º. Text deutsch und englisch. Pr. 4 M.

Einzeln (Chor I und II auf eine Stimme gedruckt.) Pr. à 1 M.

* im Sopran-, Alt-, Tenor- und Bass-Schlüssel (mit untergelegtem Klavierauszuge, nur zur etwaigen Aushülfe beim Einstudiren).

Op. 111.

Quintett

für zwei Violinen, zwei Bratschen und Violoncell.

N. Simrock in Berlin. 1891.

Verlags-Nº 9508. Partitur in 8º [Pag. 3-54] Pr. 6 M. netto.

8607

Un poco Allegretto. — **Vivace ma non troppo presto.**

Stimmen Pr. 10 M.
Für Pianoforte zu 4 Händen vom COMPONISTEN. [Pag. 2-47] 1891. Pr. 8 M.

Op. 112.

Sechs Quartette
für Sopran, Alt, Tenor und Bass mit Pianoforte.
Leipzig, C. F. Peters. 1891.
Verlags-No 7639. Edition Peters No 2646. Partitur [Pag. 3-31] Pr. 3 M. netto.

1. Sehnsucht. *(Franz Kugler.)*
Andante.

2. Nächtens. *(Franz Kugler.)*
Unruhig bewegt.

3. Vier Zigeunerlieder.
(Nach dem Ungarischen von *Hugo Conrat.*)
No 1. Allegro non troppo.

4.
No 2. Allegretto grazioso.

8607

5.

Nº 3. Allegro.

Brenn - nes-sel steht an We - ges

6.

Nº 4. Presto.

p sempre con mezza voce

Alt. Lie - be Schwal - be, klei - ne Schwal - be

pp *sempre pp*

Stimmen 8º Pr. 3 M. netto.   Einzeln (S. A. T. B.) Pr. à 75 Pf. 'n.
Nº 3-6. Vier Zigeunerlieder für eine Singstimme mit Pianoforte
übertragen von Theodor Kirchner. 1894. Text deutsch, englisch und französisch. Pr. 1 M. 50 Pf. netto.
Themata siehe oben angeführte Nummern der Partitur. (Nº 6 [Nº 4 der Zigeunerlieder] steht in *F moll*.)
(In der transponirten Ausgabe steht Nº 3 in *C dur*, Nº 4 in *D dur*, Nº 5 und 6 in *D moll*.)
Dieselben für **Pianoforte** solo übertragen von Theodor Kirchner.   Pr. 1 M. 50 Pf. netto.

Op. **113.**

13 Canons

für Frauenstimmen.

Leipzig, C. F. Peters. 1891.

Verlags-Nº 7636. Edition Peters Nº 2648. Partitur [Pag. 3-23] Pr. 2 M. 40 Pf. netto.

Nº **1.** (vierstimmig.)
(Goethe.)
Andante espressivo.
III.
Gött - li - cher

IV.
Gött - li - cher Mor-pheus, um-sonst bewegst du die lieb-

Nº **2.** (dreistimmig.)
(Goethe.)
Andante con moto.
III.
Grausam er - wei-set sich

Nº **3.** (vierstimmig.)
(Volkslied.)
Allegretto.
III. *p(cresc.)*
Sitzt a schöns

A - mor an   *p(cresc.)*

IV. *p(cresc.)*
Sitzt a schöns Vö - gerl auf'm Da - na-baum, thut nix als

No 4. (dreistimmig.)
(Volkslied.)
Andante.

No 5. (vierstimmig.)
(Volkslied.)
Allegretto.

No 6. (vierstimmig.)
(Hoffmann von Fallersleben.)
Con moto.

No 7. (dreistimmig.)
(Eichendorff.)
Andante con moto.

No 8. (vierstimmig.)
(Eichendorff.)
Risoluto.

No 9. (vierstimmig.)
(Rückert.)
Andante.

Schlaf, Kindlein, schlaf'! Der Va-ter hüt't die Schaf', die
Schlaf, Kind-lein, schaf'! Der
Wil-le wil-le will, der
Wil-le wil-le will, der Mann ist kom-men,
Mann ist kom-men, wil-le wil-le will, was bracht er denn?

So lan-ge Schönheit wird be-stehn, so lang' auf
So lan-ge
Wenn die Klänge nahn und fliehen

Ein Gems auf dem Stein, ein Vo-gel im Flug, ein Mä-del das
Ein Gems auf dem Stein, ein Vo-gel im Flug, ein
Ein

An's Au-ge des Lieb-sten fest mit Bli-cken
An's Au-ge des Lieb-sten fest mit
An's Au-ge des Lieb-sten fest mit
An's Au-ge des Lieb-sten fest

118

№ 10. (vierstimmig.) *(Rückert.)*

Andante espressivo.

Lei - se - Tö - ne der Brust, ge-weckt vom O - dem der Lie - be

№ 11. (vierstimmig.) *(Rückert.)*

Andante con moto.

Ich weiss nicht was im Hain die

Ich weiss nicht, was im Hain die Tau-be gir-ret? Ob sie be-trübt wie

№ 12. (dreistimmig.) *(Rückert.)*

Andante espressivo.

Wenn Kum-mer hät-te zu töd-ten zu töd-ten Macht__ er müss-te

№ 13. (sechsstimmig.) *(Rückert.)*

Poco Andante.

Sopran IV.

Ein-för-mig ist der Lie-be Gram,__ ein Lied ein-tö-ni-ger Wei- se.

Alt I. Ein - för - - - mig

Alt.II. Ein - - - för -

Stimmen 8º Pr. à 75 Pf.

Ausgabe mit franz. und engl. Text (ohne deutsch.)

Part. Verlags- № 7678. [Pag. 3-27] Pr. 2 M. 40 Pf. netto.

Op. 114.

Trio *(A moll)*

Für Pianoforte, Clarinette (oder Bratsche) und Violoncell.

N. Simrock in Berlin. 1892.

Verlags- № 9709. Partitur [Pag. 3-35] und Stimmen Pr. 9 M. netto.

Allegro.

Vc. Clar. poco f

poco f Pfte. un poco f

Adagio.

Clar. p dol.

Pfte. p dolce Pfte.

Clar.

Pfte.

Vc. Vc.

Andantino grazioso.

Allegro.

Für Pianoforte zu vier Händen von Paul Klengel. 1892. Pr. 6 M.

Op. 115.
Quintett
Für Clarinette (oder Bratsche), 2 Violinen, Bratsche und Violoncell.
N. Simrock in Berlin. 1892.

Verlags- No 9710, Partitur in 8º [Pag. 3-58] Pr. 6 M. netto.

Allegro.

Adagio.

120

Stimmen Preis **9** M. netto.
Für Pianoforte zu vier Händen bearbeitet von PAUL KLENGEL. 1892. Pr. 8 M.
Für 2 Pianoforte zu vier Händen bearbeitet von PAUL KLENGEL. 1892. Partitur-Ausgabe. Pr. 9 M.
Zweite Clavierstimme apart. Pr. 4 M.
Als Sonate für Violine und Pianoforte bearbeitet von PAUL KLENGEL. 1892. Pr. 8 M.
Als Duo für Clarinette und Pianoforte bearbeitet von PAUL KLENGEL. 1893. Pr. 8 M.

Op. 116.
Fantasien
für Pianoforte.
ZWEI HEFTE.

N. Simrock in Berlin. 1892.
Heft I. Verlags-№ 9874 [Pag. 3-18] Preis 4 M.
Heft II. Verlags-№ 9875 [Pag. 2-15] Preis 4 M.

HEFT I.

№ 6. Intermezzo.

Andantino teneramente.

№ 7. Capriccio.

Allegro agitato.

Für Pianoforte zu vier Händen von PAUL KLENGEL. 1893. Heft 1 u. 2 Pr. à 4 M.

№ 4. Intermezzo für Violine und Pianoforte bearbeitet von PAUL KLENGEL. 1893. Pr. 1 M. 50 Pf.
„ für Violoncell und Pianoforte bearbeitet von PAUL KLENGEL. 1893. Pr. 1 M. 50 Pf.
„ für Clarinette (oder Bratsche) und Pianoforte bearb. von PAUL KLENGEL. 1893. Pr. 1 M. 50 Pf
„ für Orchester eingerichtet von PAUL KLENGEL. 1893. Partitur Pr. 1 M. 50 Pf. netto.
Orchesterstimmen Pr. 3 M. netto.
„ für Orgel arrangirt von EDWIN H. LEMARE. 1896. Pr. 1 M. 50 Pf.
№ 6. Intermezzo für Orgel arrangirt von EDWIN H. LEMARE. 1897. Pr. 1 M. 50 Pf.

Op. 117.
Drei Intermezzi
für Pianoforte.
N. Simrock in Berlin. 1892.
Verlags-№ 9876. [Pag. 3–15] Pr. 4 M.

№ 1.

Schlaf sanft, mein Kind, schlaf sanft und schön!
Mich dauert's sehr, dich weinen sehn.
(Schottisch. Aus Herder's Volksliedern.)

Andante moderato.

№ 2.

Andante non troppo e con molto espressione.

№ 3.

Andante con moto.

molto *p* e sotto voce sempre

Für Pianoforte zu vier Händen von PAUL KLENGEL. 1893. Pr. 4 M.

№ 1 Intermezzo für Violine und Pianoforte bearbeitet von PAUL KLENGEL. 1893. Pr. 1 M. 50 Pf.

„ für Violoncell und Pianoforte bearbeitet von PAUL KLENGEL. 1893. Pr. 1 M. 50 Pf.

„ für Bratsche und Pianoforte bearbeitet von PAUL KLENGEL. 1893. Pr. 1 M. 50 Pf.

„ für Orchester eingerichtet von PAUL KLENGEL. 1893. Partitur Pr. 1 M. 50 Pf. netto.

Orchesterstimmen Pr. 3 M. netto.

„ für Orgel arrangirt von EDWIN H. LEMARE. 1897. Pr 1 M. 50 Pf.

Op. 118.

Clavierstücke.

N. Simrock in Berlin. 1893.

Verlags- № 10054 [Pag. 2-19] Pr. 4 M.

№ 1. Intermezzo.

Allegro non assai, ma molto appassionato.

f espress.

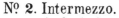

№ 2. Intermezzo.

Andante teneramente.

p *p dol.*

№ 3. Ballade.

Allegro energico.

f

№ 4. Intermezzo.
Allegretto un poco agitato.

№ 5. Romanze.
Andante.

№ 6. Intermezzo.
Andante, largo e mesto.

№ 2. Intermezzo für Violine und Pianoforte bearbeitet von RICHARD BARTH. 1894. Pr. 1 M. 50 Pf.

Op. **119**.
Clavierstücke.
N. Simrock in Berlin. 1893.
Verlags_№ 10055. [Pag. 2-19] Pr. 4 M.

№ 1. Intermezzo.
Adagio.

№ 2. Intermezzo.
Andantino un poco agitato.

No 3. Intermezzo.
Grazioso e giocoso.

No 4. Rhapsodie.
Allegro risoluto.

Op. 120.
Zwei Sonaten
Für Clarinette (oder Bratsche) und Pianoforte.
N. Simrock in Berlin. 1895.

No I. Verlags- No 10408 [Pag. 3-30] Pr. 8 M.
No II. Verlags- No 10409 [Pag. 3-30] Pr. 8 M.
Bratschen-Stimmen apart. Pr. a 2 M.

No 1.

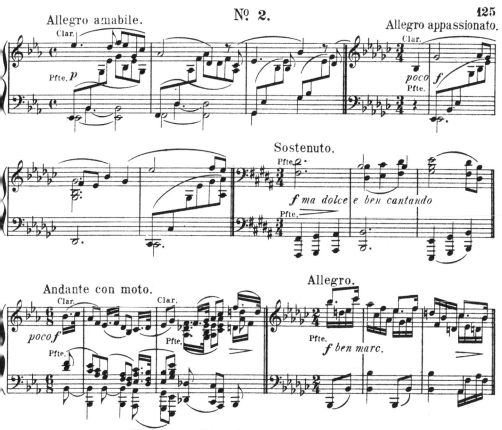

Allegro amabile. ... Allegro appassionato.

Sostenuto.

Andante con moto. ... Allegro.

Ausgabe für Violine und Pianoforte vom COMPONISTEN. 1895. Pr. à 8 M.
Für Pianoforte zu vier Händen bearbeitet von PAUL KLENGEL. 1895. Pr. à 6 M.

Op. 121.

Vier ernste Gesänge

für eine Bassstimme mit Begleitung des Pianoforte.

English text adapted by *Paul England.*

Max Klinger zugeeignet.

N. Simrock in Berlin. 1896.
Verlags-N⁰ 10679 [Pag. 3-19] Pr. 4 M.

N⁰ 1. (Prediger Salomo, Cap. 3.)
Ecclesiastes, III.
Andante.

Denn es ge-het dem Men-schen wie dem
One thing be-falleth the beasts and the sons of

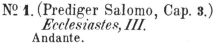

Nº 2. (Prediger Salomo, Cap. 4.)
Ecclesiastes, IV.
Andante.

Ich wand - te mich und sa - he
So I re - turn'd and did con -

Nº 3. (Jesus Sirach, Cap. 41.)
Ecclesiasticus, 41.
Grave.

O Tod, o Tod, wie bit - ter, wie bit _
O death, O death, how bit - ter, how bit _

Nº 4.(S. Pauli an die Corinther I., Cap. 13.)
I. Corinthians, XIII.
Andante con moto ed anima.

Wenn ich mit Men - schen und mit
Though I speak with the tongues of

Ausgabe für Alt oder Baryton 1896. Pr 4 M.
(Die **Tonarten** sind dieselben wie in der **Original-Ausgabe**. Die **Singstimme** steht im Schlüssel eine Octave tiefer.)

Ausgabe für Sopran oder Tenor. 1896. Pr. 4 M.
(Nº 1 steht in *F moll*, Nº 2 in *B moll*, Nº 3 in *G moll* und Nº 4 in *G dur*.)

Werke ohne Opuszahl.
51 Uebungen
für das Pianoforte.
ZWEI HEFTE.

N. Simrock in Berlin. 1893.
Heft I. Verlags-N° 10062 [Pag. 2-27] Pr. 3 M. netto.
Heft II. Verlags-N° 10065 [Pag. 2-27] Pr. 3 M. netto.

HEFT I.

128

*) Die eingeklammerten Noten (o) werden nicht angeschlagen, sondern nur während der Uebung ausgehalten.

8607

Album

für Violoncell mit Begleitung des Pianoforte.

Herausgegeben von NORBERT SALTER.

N. Simrock in Berlin. 1896.

Verlags No 10744 [Pag. 3–14] Pr. 2 M. 40 Pfge. netto.

(No 1. Feldeinsamkeit. — No 2. „Wie Melodien zieht es mir." — No 3. Sapphische Ode. — No 4. Wiegenlied. — No 5. Liebestreu. — No 6. Minnelied.)

Ausgewählte Lieder

für eine Singstimme mit Begleitung des Pianoforte.

(Innerer Titel Original-Zeichnung von *Max Klinger*.)

N. Simrock in Berlin.

Band   I.   Verlags-No 9194. [Pag. 3–39] Pr. 3 M. netto.
Band II.   Verlags-No 9199. [Pag. 3–30] Pr. 3 M. netto.
Band III.   Verlags-No 9214. [Pag. 3–31] Pr. 3 M. netto.
Band IV.   Verlags-No 9216. [Pag. 3–31] Pr. 3 M. netto.
Band   V.   Verlags-No 9574. [Pag. 3–31] Pr. 3 M. netto.
Band VI.   Verlags-No 9576. [Pag. 3–31] Pr. 3 M. netto.
Band VII.   Verlags-No 9578. [Pag. 3–31] Pr. 3 M. netto.

(BAND I. No 1. Liebestreu. — No 2. An ein Veilchen. — No 3. „Meine Liebe ist grün –" No 4. Alte Liebe. — No 5. An die Nachtigall. — No 6. Feldeinsamkeit. — BAND II. No 1. Sapphische Ode. — No 2. Botschaft. — No 3. Vergebliches Ständchen. — No 4. Der Gang zum Liebchen. – No 5. Sommerabend. — No 6. „Dort in den Weiden –" BAND III. No 1. Wiegenlied. — No 2. Minnelied. — No 3. Sonntag. — No 4. An den Mond. — No 5. Geheimniss. — No 6. An eine Aeolsharfe. — BAND IV. No 1. Am Sonntag Morgen. — No 2. Treue Liebe. — No 3. Der Schmied. — No 4. Des Liebsten Schwur. — No 5. „O wüsst' ich doch den Weg zurück –" No 6. „Ich sah als Knabe Blumen blüh'n –" BAND V. No 1. Therese. — No 2. Die Kränze. — No 3. „O liebliche Wangen –" No 4. Erinnerung. — No 5. In Waldeseinsamkeit. — No 6. Mädchenlied. — BAND VI. No 1. „Wir wandelten, wir zwei zusammen –" No 2. Der Jäger. — No 3. Meerfahrt. — No 4. Komm' bald – No 5. Trennung. — No 6. „Bei dir sind meine Gedanken –" BAND VII. No 1. Ständchen. — No 2. Der Kranz. – No 3. „O kühler Wald –" No 4. Auf dem Schiffe. – No 5. Beim Abschied. — No 6. „Der Tod, das ist' die kühle Nacht –")

Ausgabe für tiefe Stimme. Pr. à 3 M. netto.

Deutsche Volkslieder
mit Clavier-Begleitung.

(Heft 1–6 für eine Singstimme, Heft 7 für Vorsänger und kleinen Chor.)

N. Simrock in Berlin. 1894.

Heft 1. Verlags-№ 10206. [Pag. 4–15] Pr. 4 M.
Heft 2. Verlags-№ 10207. [Pag. 3–19] Pr. 4 M.
Heft 3. Verlags-№ 10208. [Pag. 3–15] Pr. 4 M.
Heft 4. Verlags-№ 10209. [Pag. 3–19] Pr. 4 M.
Heft 5. Verlags-№ 10210. [Pag. 3–19] Pr. 4 M.
Heft 6. Verlags-№ 10211. [Pag. 3–15] Pr. 4 M.
Heft 7. (Partitur) Verlags-№ 10218. [Pag. 3–18] Pr. 4 M.

Vorsängerstimme Pr. 1 M. Chorstimmen Pr. 2 M. Einzeln (Sopran Alt Tenor und Bass) Pr. à 50 Pf.

HEFT I.

№ 1. „Sagt mir, o schönste Schäf'rin mein —"

Zärtlich und lebhaft.

№ 2. „Erlaube mir, fein's —"
Zart.

№ 3. „Gar lieblich hat sich —"
Anmuthig.

№ 4. „Guten Abend —"
Drängend, doch nicht schnell.

№ 5. „Die Sonne scheint —"
Gehalten und empfindungsvoll.

HEFT IV.

8607

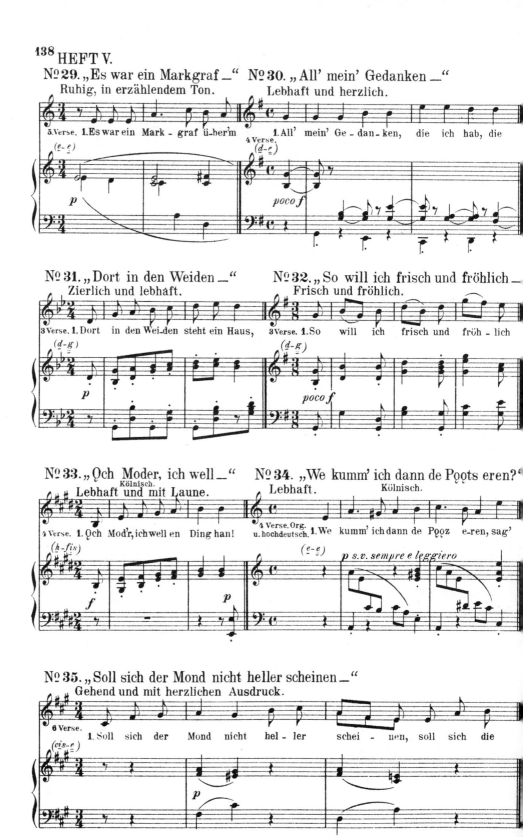

Diese Lieder können durchaus auch ohne Clavier gesungen werden.

Ausgabe für tiefe Stimme (Heft 1–6) 1894. Pr. à 4 M.

(Nº 1 und 39 stehen in *A dur*, Nº 2. 3. 7. 8. 11. 13. 20. 22. 24. 26 und 30 in *F dur*, Nº 4. 14. 15. 29. 34. 36. 38 und 40 in *G moll*, Nº 5 und 32 in *E dur*, Nº 6. 18 und 27 in *Es dur*, Nº 9. 16. 33 und 42 in *D dur*, Nº 10 in *H moll*, Nº 17. 31. 35 und 37 in *E moll*, Nº 19 und 41 in *As dur*, Nº 21 und 28 in *C moll*, Nº 12 und 23 in *A moll* und Nº 25 in *G dur*.)

German Folk-Songs. 1894. Text englisch und deutsch. English version by *Albert I. Bach*. Themata etc. wie die deutsche Ausgabe.

Für drei Frauenstimmen mit Begleitung des Pianoforte eingerichtet von FRIEDRICH HEGAR. 1897. Nº 1 (Orig. Ausg. Nº 1) Nº 2 (Orig. Ausg. Nº 3) Nº 3 (Orig. Ausg. Nº 5) Nº 4 (Orig. Ausg. Nº 8) Nº 5 (Orig. Ausg. Nº 9) Nº 6 (Orig. Ausg. Nº 15) Nº 7 (Orig. Ausg. Nº 16) Nº 8 (Orig. Ausg. Nº 20) Nº 9 (Orig. Ausg. Nº 22) Nº 10 (Orig. Ausg. Nº 23) Nº 11 (Orig. Ausg. Nº 24) Nº 12 (a Capella, steht in *As dur*) (Orig. Ausg. Nº 6). **Partitur** in 8º Preis à 1 M. **Singstimmen** Preis à 90 Pf. Einzeln jede à 30 Pf.

Für Männerchor a Capella eingerichtet von FRIEDRICH HEGAR. 1897. 4 Hefte. Partitur 8º Pr. à 1 M. 50 Pf. Singstimmen 8º Pr. à 3 M. 20 Pf. Einzeln: Tenor I, II, Bass I, II, Pr à 80 Pf. für jedes Heft. (Heft I. enthält Nº 2. 3. 4. 5. 6. 8., Heft II. Nº 10. 13. 17. 19. 22. 23., Heft III. Nº 24. 25. 26. 29. 30. 31. u. Heft IV. Nº 32. 36. 37. 39. 41. 42 der Orig. Ausgabe.)

(Nº 2. 6. 8. 24 und 30 stehen in *B dur*, Nº 3. 22 und 26 in *A dur*, Nº 4. 23. 29 und 36 in *C moll*, Nº 13 in *F dur*, Nº 25 und 37 in *C dur*, Nº 32 in *As dur*, Nº 39 in *Es dur*, Nº 41 in *D dur* und Nº 42 in *G dur*.)

Mondnacht.

Gedicht von *Joseph von Eichendorff*

für eine Singstimme mit Begleitung des Pianoforte.

Raabe & Plothow (vorm. Luckhardt'sche
Musik-Verlagshandlung) Berlin. 1872.

Verlags-No.C.L. **686.** [Pag. **2—3.**] Preis **80** Pf.

Zuerst erschienen 1854 in „Albumblätter." 8 Lieder mit Pianof. Göttingen bei G.H.Wigand.

Ausgabe für hohe Stimme. *B dur.* Pr. **80** Pf.
Ausgabe für tiefe Stimme. *F dur.* Pr. **80** Pf.

Deutsche Volkslieder

für vierstimmigen Chor gesetzt.

(Sopran, Alt, Tenor, Bass.)

Der *Wiener Singacademie* gewidmet.

Leipzig und Winterthur, J.Rieter-Biedermann. 1864.

Heft I. Verlags-No 395ᵃ Partitur in 8º [Pag. **4—19.**] Preis **1 M. 50** Pf.
Heft II. Verlags-No 395ᵇ Partitur in 8º [Pag. **4—19.**] Preis **1 M. 50** Pf.

HEFT I.

No 1.
Von edler Art.

No 2.
Mit Lust thät ich ausreiten.

No 3.
Bei nächtlicher Weil.

142 N⁰ 4.

Vom heiligen Märtyrer Emmerano, Bischoffen zu Regensburg.

N⁰ 5.
Täublein weiss.

N⁰ 6.
Ach lieber Herre Jesu Christ.

N⁰ 7.
Sankt Raphael.

HEFT II. N⁰ 1.
In stiller Nacht.

N⁰ 2.
Abschiedslied.

N⁰ 3.
Der todte Knabe.

N⁰ 4.
Die Wollust in den Mayen.

N⁰ 5.
Morgengesang.

N⁰ 6.
Schnitter Tod.

N⁰ 7.
Der englische Jäger.

Stimmen in 8° Heft I.II. Preis à 2 M.
Einzeln: Sopran, Alt, Tenor, Bass Pr. à 50 Pf. für jedes Heft.

8607

Volks-Kinderlieder

mit hinzugefügter Clavierbegleitung.

Den Kindern *Robert* und *Clara Schumann's* gewidmet.

(Ohne Namen des Autors.)

Leipzig und Winterthur, J. Rieter-Biedermann. 1858.

Verlags-No 60. [Pag. 2—19.] Preis 3 M.

Nº 7.

Das Schlaraffenland.

Fool's paradise.

Allegro.

Nº 8ª (Plattdeutsch) und **Nº 8ᵇ** (Hochdeutsch.)

Beim Ritt auf dem Knie.

The ride on the knee.

Allegretto. (*g-es*)

(*d-f*) In Po-len steht ein Haus, in
As I have heard them tell, as

8ª. Ull Mann wull ri-den, wull hat he keen Pärd;
8ᵇ. Alt' Mann wollt' rei-ten und hat-te kein Pferd;
He would go ri-ding but no horse had he

Nº 9.

Der Jäger im Walde.

The huntsman.

Allegro.

Nº 10.

Das Mädchen und die Hasel.

The maiden and the hazel.

Allegretto.

(*c-g*) Der Jä-ger in dem Wal-de sich
The huntsman seeks the fo-rest and

(*c-f*) Es wollt' ein Mädchen brechen geh'n die
A-long the fields a maiden went, to

Nº 11.

Wiegenlied.

Cradlesong.

Con moto.

(*g-g*) Schlaf, Kindlein, schlaf'! Der Va-ter hüt't die Schaaf, die Mut-ter
Sleep, ba-by, sleep, while fa-ther keeps the sheep, and mo-ther

№ 12.

Weihnachten.

Christmas carol.

Con moto.

№ 13.

Marienwürmchen.

Ladybird.

Andante.

№ 14.

Dem Schutzengel.

The guardian Angel.

Andante.

Originalausgabe

Einzeln: № 1 und 2 zusammen Pr. 70 Pf. № 3. 4. 7. 10. Pr. a 70 Pf.
№ 5 und 6, № 8 und 9, № 11 und 12, № 13 und 14. Preis à 70 Pf.

Popular Nursery Songs with additional Pianoforte accompaniment.

English version by *Miss E.M.Traquair.*

(Dedicated to the children of *Robert* and *Clara Schumann*) gr. 8° 1872. Preis **3 M.**

Einzeln: № 1. The sleeping Beauty in the wood. Pr. 50 Pf.

2. Henny Penny. (Orig. № 3.) Pr. 50 Pf.

3. The little Dustman. (Orig. № 4.) Pr. 50 Pf.

4. 5. The nightingale. (Orig. № 2.) Some one. Pr. 50 Pf.

6. 7. The bonny Rosebud. Fool's paradise. Pr. 50 Pf.

8. 9. The ride on the knee. The huntsman. Pr. 50 Pf.

10. The maiden and the hazel. Pr. 50 Pf.

11. 12. Cradlesong. Christmas carol. Pr. 50 Pf.

13. 14. Ladybird. The guardian Angel. Pr. 50 Pf.

№ 4. (Sandmännchen) Für Pianoforte allein von THEODOR KIRCHNER. 1878. Preis **1 M. 50 Pf.**

Choralvorspiel und Fuge

für Orgel

über „O Traurigkeit, o Herzeleid."

Leipzig, E. W. Fritzsch.

Beilage zum 13. Jahrgang (1881) des „Musikalischen Wochenblattes."

[Pag. 2—7.] Preis 1 M. 50 Pf.

Choralvorspiel.

Poco Adagio.

(17 Takte)

Fuge.

Adagio.

Fuge *(As moll)*

für die Orgel componirt.

N. Simrock in Berlin.

Beilage zu der Allgemeinen musikalischen Zeitung 1864. N⁰ 29.

Neue Ausgabe 1883. Verlags-N⁰ 9020. [Pag. 3—7.] Preis 1 M. 50 Pf.

Langsam.

Studien

für das Pianoforte.

Leipzig, Bartholf Senff. I. II. 1869. III. IV. V. 1879.

I. Etude nach *Fr. Chopin.* Verlags-N⁰ 884. [Pag. 2—7.] Preis 1 M. 50 Pf.

II. Rondo nach *C. M. v. Weber.* Verlags-N⁰ 885. [Pag. 2—15.] Preis 2 M.

I. II. in einem Heft. Verlags-N⁰ 886. [Pag. 2—21.] Preis 3 M.

III. Presto nach *J. S. Bach.* Verlags-N⁰ 1393. [Pag. 2—5.] Preis 1 M.

IV. Presto nach *J. S. Bach.* 2ᵗᵉ Bearbeitung. Verlags-N⁰ 1394. [Pag. 2—5.] Preis 1 M.

V. Chaconne nach *J. S. Bach.* Verlags-N⁰ 1395. [Pag. 2—15.] Preis 2 M.

I.

Etude nach Fr. Chopin.

Poco presto.

II.
Rondo nach C. M. von Weber.

III.
Presto nach J. S. Bach.
Erste Bearbeitung.

IV.
Presto nach J. S. Bach.
Zweite Bearbeitung.

V.
Chaconne von J. S. Bach.
Für die linke Hand allein bearbeitet.

Gavotte
von C. W. Gluck.
Für das Pianoforte gesetzt
und Frau *Clara Schumann* zugeeignet.
Leipzig, Bartholf Senff. 1871.

Verlags-No 1105. Zum Concertvortrag. [Pag. 2—5.] Preis 1 M.

Gavotte. (Aus Iphigenie in Aulis.)
Grazioso.

Für Pianoforte leicht spielbar bearbeitet. Pr. 50 Pf.
Für Pianoforte zu 4 Händen bearbeitet. Pr. 1 M.

Ungarische Tänze

für das Pianoforte zu vier Händen gesetzt.

N. Simrock in Berlin. Heft I. II. März 1869. Heft III. IV. 1880.

Heft I.   Verlags-No 6998. [Pag 2—29.] Preis 4 M. 50 Pf.
Heft II. Verlags-No 6999. [Pag 2—29.] Preis 4 M. 50 Pf.
Heft III. Verlags-No 8167. [Pag 2—31.] Preis 4 M. 50 Pf.
Heft IV. Verlags-No 8168. [Pag 2—27.] Preis 4 M. 50 Pf.

HEFT I.

HEFT IV.

Originalausgabe. Heft I — IV. Pr. à 4 M. 50 Pf.
Neue Prachtausgabe in 1 Band. [Pag. 2 – 95.] Pr. 10 M. netto.
Ausgabe in 2 Bänden. (Ed. Peters № 2100 a b) Pr. pro Band 6 M. netto.

Arrangements:

Leichtes Arrangement für Pianoforte zu 4 Händen. Nach Belieben auch ohne Octavenspannungen
zu spielen mit Bezeichnung des Fingersatzes von ROBERT KELLER.

Heft I. 1876. № 1. (2 der Orig. Ausgabe) № II. (3 der Orig. Ausg.) № III. (4 der Orig. Ausg.)
in G moll. Pr. 2 M. 50 Pf.

Heft II. 1876. № IV. (5 d. Orig. Ausg.) in A moll. № V. (7 d. Orig. Ausg.) in B dur. № VI.
(6 d. Orig. Ausg.) in C dur. Pr. 2 M. 50 Pf.

Heft III. 1881. № VII. (12 d. Orig. Ausg.) № VIII. (15 d. Orig. Ausg.) in A dur. № IX. (13 d.
Orig. Ausg.) in C dur. № X. (16 d. Orig. Ausg.) in G moll. Pr. 2 M. 50 Pf.

Heft IV. 1881. № XI. (17 d. Orig. Ausg.) in A moll. № XII. (18 d. Orig. Ausg.) in C dur.
№ XIII. (20 d. Orig. Ausg.) № XIV. (21 d. Orig. Ausg.). Pr. 2 M. 50 Pf.

Für Pianoforte zu zwei Händen gesetzt vom COMPONISTEN. Heft I. [Pag. 2—23.] II. [Pag. 2—23.] 1872.
(№ 4 in Fis moll, № 7 in F dur) Pr. à Heft 3 M. 50 Pf.

Heft III. IV. gesetzt von THEODOR KIRCHNER. 1881. Pr. à 3 M. 50 Pf.
Neue Prachtausgabe in 1 Band. Preis 7 M. 50 Pf. netto.
Ausgabe in 2 Bänden (Ed. Peters № 2101 a b) Preis pro Band 4 M. netto.

Für Pianoforte zu 2 Händen in erleichterter Spielart von ROBERT KELLER.
(Edition facilité) Heft I. II. 1876. Heft III. IV. 1881. Pr. à Heft 3 M.

Für Pianoforte zu 6 Händen arrangirt von ROBERT KELLER. 1877.
Heft I. № 1. 2. d. Orig. Ausg. Heft II. № 3. 4. 5. d. Orig. Ausg.
Heft III. № 6. 7. 9. d. Orig. Ausg. Heft IV. № 8. 10. d. Orig. Ausg. Preis à Heft 2 M.

Für zwei Pianoforte zu 4 Händen von ROBERT KELLER. 1890. № 1. Pr. 3 M.; № 2-7. Pr. à 2 M.;
№ 8. Pr. 3 M.; № 9. (Orig. Ausg. № 13), № 10. (Orig. Ausg. № 15), № 11. (Orig. Ausg. № 17),
№ 12. (Orig. Ausg. № 18), № 13. (Orig. Ausg. № 20) und № 14. (Orig. Ausg. № 21), Pr. à 2 M.

Für zwei Pianoforte zu 8 Händen von ROBERT KELLER. Heft I. II. 1874. Heft III. IV. 1881. Pr. à Heft 8 M.

Für Pianoforte und Violine von JOSEPH JOACHIM. Heft I.II. 1871. Heft III. IV. 1880. (N⁰ 4. *H moll.*
N⁰ 5. *G moll.* N⁰ 6. *B dur.* N⁰ 10. *G dur.* N⁰ 15. *A dur.*
N⁰ 16. *G moll.* N⁰ 19. *A moll.* N⁰ 20. *D moll.*) Pr. à Heft 5 M.

Für Pianoforte und Violine in leichtem Arrangement von FRIEDR. HERMANN. Pr. à Heft 3 M.
Heft I.II. 1878. Heft III. IV. 1880.
(Heft I enthält: N⁰ 1. 3. 5., Heft II. N⁰ 6. 7. 8., Heft III. N⁰ 11. 13. 14. 15.,
Heft IV. N⁰ 17. 20. 18 der Orig. Ausg.)
(N⁰ 5 steht in *G moll,* N⁰ 6 in *D dur,* N⁰ 15 in *A dur* und N⁰ 20 in *D moll.*)

Für Pianoforte und Violoncell von ALFREDO PIATTI. Heft I—IV. 1881. Pr. à Heft 5 M. (N⁰ 4. *D moll.*
N⁰ 5. *F moll.* N⁰ 6 und N⁰ 7. *C dur.* N⁰ 9. *D moll.* N⁰ 10. *C dur.*
N⁰ 16. *C moll.* N⁰ 17. *E moll.* N⁰ 19. *D moll.* N⁰ 21. *D moll.*)

Für Pianoforte, Violine und Violoncell von FRIEDR. HERMANN. 1890. N⁰ 1-6. Pr. à 2 M.
N⁰ 7. Pr. 1 M. 50 Pf.; N⁰ 8. Pr. 2 M.; N⁰ 9. (Orig. Ausg. N⁰ 13), Pr. 1 M. 50 Pf.;
N⁰ 10. (Orig. Ausg. N⁰ 15), N⁰ 11. (Orig. Ausg. N⁰ 17.), N⁰ 12. (Orig. Ausg. N⁰ 18.),
N⁰ 13. (Orig. Ausg. N⁰ 20.) und N⁰ 14. (Orig. Ausg. N⁰ 21.), Pr. à 2 M.

Für Pianoforte zu 4 Händen mit Violine und Violoncell von FRIEDR. HERMANN. Heft I-IV. Pr. à Hft. 6 M.
(N⁰ 5 steht in *G moll.* N⁰ 6 in *D dur* und N⁰ 17 in *F moll.*)

Für Pianoforte und Flöte von FRIEDR. HERMANN. N⁰ 1. 2. Pr. à 1 M. N⁰ 3. Pr. 80 Pf.
N⁰ 4. (Orig. Ausg. N⁰ 5) Pr. 1 M. N⁰ 5. (Orig. A. N⁰ 6) in *D dur.* Pr 1 M.
N⁰ 6. (Orig. Ausg. N⁰ 7) Pr. 80 Pf. N⁰ 7. (Orig. A. N⁰ 9) Pr. 80 Pf.
N⁰ 8. (Orig. Ausg. N⁰ 8) Pr. 1 M.

Für Pianoforte, Flöte und Violine (oder Pianoforte und 2 Flöten) von FRIEDR. HERMANN.
(Nummern und Tonarten wie für Pianoforte und Flöte) 1875.
N⁰ 1. 2. 4. 5. 8. Pr. à 1 M. 30 Pf. N⁰ 3. 6. 7. Pr. à 1 M.

Für 2 Violinen von FRIEDR. HERMANN. (N⁰ 1. 2. 3. 5. *G moll.* N⁰ 6. *D dur.* 7. 8. d. Orig. Ausg.) Partiturausg. Pr. à 4 M.

Für Orchester gesetzt vom COMPONISTEN. N⁰ 1. 3. 10 (in *F dur*) d. Orig. Ausg. 1874.
Partitur in 8⁰. [Pag. 1—60] Pr. 9 M. netto.
Orchesterstimmen (Piccolo, 2 Fl., 2 Ob., 2 Clar., 2 Fag., 4 Hörner, 2 Tromp., Pauken,
Triangel, Gr. Cassa e Piatti, Streichorch.) Pr. 15 M.
Einzeln: Viol. I., II., Bratsche, Violoncell, Bass. Preis à 1 M.

Für Orchester gesetzt von ANDREAS HALLÉN. N⁰ 2 und 7 d. Orig. Ausg. 1894.
Partitur in 8⁰ [Pag. 3-34] Pr. 4 M. 50 Pf. netto.
Orchesterstimmen (2 Fl., 2 Ob., 2 Clar., 2 Fag., 4 Hörner, 2 Tromp., 3 Posaunen,
Pauken, kl. Trommel u. Streichorchester) Pr. 9 M.
Einzeln: Viol. I, II und Bratsche Pr. à 80 Pf., Vcell., C. Bass Pr. à 50 Pf.

Für Orchester gesetzt von ALBERT PARLOW: N⁰ 5 und 6 d. Orig. Ausg. (N⁰ 5 in *G moll* N⁰ 6 in *D dur*) 1876.
Partitur in 8⁰ Pr. 5 M.
Orchesterstimmen (Piccolo, Gr. Flöte, 2 Ob., 2 Clar., 2 Fag., 4 Hörner, 2 Tromp.,
3 Posaunen, Pauken u. Streichorchester) Pr. 9 M.
Einzeln: Viol. I., II., Br., Vcell., C. Bass. Pr. à 80 Pf.
Drittes Heft der Orig. Ausgabe (N⁰ 11—16) 1881.
Partitur in 8⁰ [Pag. 5—95] Pr. 15 M. netto.
Orchesterstimmen (Piccolo, 2 Fl., 2 Ob., 2 Clar., 2 Fag., 4 Hörner, 2 Tromp.,
3 Posaunen, Pauken, Harfe u. Streichorchester) Pr. 18 M.
Einzeln: Viol. I. II., Br. Pr. à 1 M. 50 Pf. Vcell. u. C. Bass. Pr. 2 M.

Für Orchester gesetzt von ANTON DVOŘÁK: Viertes Heft der Orig. Ausgabe (N⁰ 17—21) 1881.
Partitur in 8⁰ [Pag. 5—80] Pr. 15 M. netto.
Orchesterstimmen (Piccolo, 2 Fl., 2 Ob., 2 Clar., 2 Fag., 4 Hörner, 2 Tromp.,
3 Pos., Pauken, Triangel, Gr. Trommel und Becken,
Harfe ad libitum, Streichorchester) Pr. 18 M.
Einzeln: Viol. I., II., Br. Pr. à 1 M. Vcell. und C. Bass. Pr. 2 M.

Für Orgel arrangirt von EDWIN H. LEMARE. 1896. N⁰ 1 und 5. Pr. a 1 M. 50 Pf.

Zigeunerlied *(Gipsey Song)*: „Wir leben nur von heut auf morgen" *"We live to-day".* Deutsche Uebersetz.
nach dem Französischen des Victor Wilder von Frau *Malybrok-Stieler.* English version by Mrs. *John P. Morgan.*
Duett für zwei Singstimmen mit Begleitung des Pianoforte nach
den Ungarischen Tänzen N⁰ 6 und 5 von JOHANNES BRAHMS arrangirt von PAULINE VIARDOT. 1886.
[Zuerst: Les Bohémiennes (Text französisch und spanisch). Paris, J. Hamelle.]

II.

Verzeichnisse und Register.

1. Systematisches Verzeichniss,

nach den

Organen der Ausführung

geordnet.

I. Instrumentalmusik.

D. Für Orgel.

II. Gesangsmusik.

A. Gesänge ohne Begleitung.

1. Gesänge für gemischten Chor.

2. Gesänge für Frauenchor.

3. Gesänge für Männerchor.

B. Gesänge mit Begleitung.

1. Gesangswerke mit Orchester.

2. Gesänge mit Begleitung mehrerer In-strumente.

3. Gesänge mit Begleitung der Orgel oder des Pianoforte.

4. Gesänge mit Begleitung des Pianoforte.

a) Chöre.

b) Solo-Quartette.

c) Duette.

2. Alphabetisches Register
der Ueberschriften und Textanfänge sämmtlicher Gesangswerke.

Anhang.

a) Systematische Uebersicht

der

Arrangements und Bearbeitungen.

A. Für Orchester.

1) Für grosses Orchester.

Intermezzo. Op. 116, No. 4. (*Paul Klengel.*)
—— Op. 117, No. 1. (*Paul Klengel.*)
Ungarische Tänze. Heft I, No. *1. 2. *3. 5.
Heft II, No. 6, 7. *10. Heft III, No. 11—16.
Heft IV, No. 17—21. S. 151.

2) Für Streichorchester.

Liebeslieder. Walzer. Op. 52. (*Friedr. Hermann.*)

3) Für Militair-Musik.

Akademische Fest - Ouvertüre. Op. 80. (*A. Reindel.*)

B. Für 2 Violinen.

Liebeslieder. Walzer. Op. 52.
Ungarische Tänze. No. 1—3. 5—8. S. 151.

C. Für Pianoforte.

1) Mit Violine und Violoncell.

*Concert für Violine und Violoncell. Op. 102.
Sextett. Op. 18 als Trio. (*Th. Kirchner.*)
Sextett. Op. 36 als Trio. (*Th. Kirchner.*)
Ungarische Tänze. No. 1—8. 13. 15. 17. 18.
20. 21. (*Fr. Hermann.*) S. 151.

2) Mit Violine und Flöte oder 2 Flöten.

Liebeslieder. Walzer. Op. 52.
Ungarische Tänze. No. 1—3. 5—9. S. 151.
Wiegenlied. Op. 49, No. 4.

3) Mit Violine.

Intermezzo. Op. 116, No. 4. Op. 117, No. 1.
(*Paul Klengel.*)
—— Op. 118, No. 2. (*Richard Barth.*)
Liebeslieder. Walzer. Op. 52.
Menuett I, II aus Op. 11.
Quintett. Op. 115. (*Paul Klengel.*)
*Sonaten für Clarinette. Op. 120, No. 1. 2.

Ungarische Tänze. Heft I—IV. (*Jos. Joachim.*)
S. 151.
—— Auswahl, leicht. Heft I bis IV. (*Fr. Hermann*). S. 151.
Wiegenlied. Op. 49, No. 4.
Walzer. Op. 39 (4 händig mit Violine.)

4) Mit Violoncell.

Album (*Norbert Salter.*) S. 133.
Intermezzo. Op. 116, No. 4; Op. 117, No. 1.
(*Paul Klengel.*)
Sonate für Violine. Op. 78. (*Paul Klengel.*)
Ungarische Tänze. Heft I—IV. (*Alfr. Piatti.*)
S. 151.

5) Mit Flöte.

Liebeslieder. Walzer. Op. 52.
Ungarische Tänze. No. 1—3. 5—9. S. 151.
Wiegenlied. Op. 49, No. 4.

6) Mit Clarinette (od. Bratsche.)

Intermezzo. Op. 116, No. 4; Op. 117, No. 1.
(*Paul Klengel.*)
Quintett. Op. 115. (*Paul Klengel.*)

7) Mit Harmonium.

Adagio aus Op. 78. (*Aug. Reinhard.*)
Allegro amabile aus Op. 100. (*Aug. Reinhard.*)

8) Zu 4 Händen mit Violine und Violoncell.

Liebeslieder. Walzer. Op. 52.
Quartette. Op. 25. 26. 51 (No. 1. 2). 60. 67.
Quintett. Op. 34.
Serenade. Op. 16.
Sextette. Op. 18. 36.
Symphonien. Op. 68. 73. 90. 98.
Ungarische Tänze. Heft I—IV. S. 151.
Walzer. Op. 39.

9) Für 2 Pianoforte zu 8 Händen.

Concert für Pianoforte. Op. 15.
Serenaden. Op. 11. 16.
Symphonien. Op. 68. 73. 90. 98.
Ouvertüren. Op. 80. 81.
Ungarische Tänze. Heft I—IV. S. 150.

---

*) Arrangement vom Componisten.

10) Für 2 Pianoforte zu 4 Händen.

*Concert (D moll). Op. 15.
* —— (B dur). Op. 83.
Quartette. Op. 25. 26. 60.
Quintett. Op. 115.
Serenaden. Op. 11. 16.
Sextett. Op. 18.
Symphonien. Op. 68. 73.
* —— Op. 90. 98.
Ungarische Tänze. No. 1—8. 13. 15. 17. 18.
 20. 21. S. 150.
Variationen. Op. 23. 24. 56 b.

11) Zu 6 Händen.

Liebeslieder. Walzer. Op. 52.
Ungarische Tänze. No. 1—10. S. 150.
Wiegenlied. Op. 49, No. 4.

12) Zu 4 Händen.

Ave Maria. Op. 12.
Balladen. Op. 10.
Begräbnissgesang. Op. 13.
*Concert für Pianoforte. Op. 15.
 —— für Pianoforte. Op. 83.
 —— für Violine. Op. 77.
 —— für Violine und Violoncell. Op. 102.
Fantasien. Op. 116. 2 Hefte. (Paul Klengel.)
Gavotte von Gluck. Ohne Op. S. 147.
Gesänge für Frauenchor. Op. 17.
 —— für gemischten Chor. Op. 42.
Gesang der Parzen. Op. 89.
Intermezzi. Op. 117. (Paul Klengel.)
Liebeslieder. Op. 52 a. 65.
*Ouvertüren. Op. 80. 81.
*Quartette. Op. 25. 26. 51, I. II.
Quartett. Op. 60.
* —— Op. 67.
Quintett. Op. 34.
*Quintette. Op. 88. 111.
Quintett. Op. 115.
*Requiem. Op. 45.
Rhapsodie. Op. 53.
Rinaldo. Op. 50.
Scherzo. Op. 4.
Schicksalslied. Op. 54.
*Serenaden. Op. 11. 16.
*Sextette. Op. 18. 36.
Sonaten für Pianoforte. Op. 1. 2. (Paul Klengel.)
 —— für Violine. Op. 78. 100. 108. (Rob.
 Keller.)
 —— für Violoncell. Op. 38. 99. (Robert
 Keller.)
 —— für Clarinette. Op. 120, No. 1. 2.
 (Paul Klengel.)
*Symphonien. Op. 68. 73. 90. 98.
Trios. Op. 8. 40. 87. 101. 114.
*Triumphlied. Op. 55.
Ungarische Tänze, leichte Auswahl. 4 Hefte.
 S. 150.
Variationen. Op. 21, I. II. 24. 56.
Walzer. Op. 39.
Wiegenlied. Op. 49, No. 4.
Zigeunerlieder. Op. 103. (Theod. Kirchner.)

13) Zu 2 Händen.

Brahms - Album. Gesänge von Johannes
 Brahms. Bearbeitung für Pianoforte. Mit
 untergelegtem deutschen und engl. Text.
 N. Simrock in Berlin 1883. Preis à Band
 5 Mark.
  Bd. I: Op. 19. 46—49. 69.
  „ II: Op. 70—72. 85. 86.
  „ III: Op. 20. 61. 66. 75, No. 2. 3.
   Op. 84. 62.
Duette. Op. 75, No. 3 und Brahms-Album
 Band III.
Gavotte von Gluck. Leicht spielbar. S. 111.
Gesang der Parzen. Op. 89.
Liebeslieder. Op. 52. 65.
Lieder für gemischten Chor. Op. 62.
Lieder und Gesänge. Op. 3. 7. 14, No. 4 u. 7.
 Op. 32, No. 9. Op. 33, No. 3. 5. 9. 12. 14.
 Op. 43, No. 1. 2. 4. Op. 47, No. 3. Op. 49,
 No. 2. 4. Op. 57, No. 2. 3. 6. Op. 58,
 No. 3. 4. 5. 8. Op. 59, No. 2. 5. 8. Op. 69,
 No. 3. 4. Op. 71, No. 5. Op. 72, No. 1.
 Op. 84, No. 4. Sandmännchen. Brahms-
 Album Bd. I. II.
Ouvertüren. Op. 80. 81.
Quartette. Op. 51, I. II. 67. (Paul Klengel.)
Requiem. Op. 45.
Rinaldo. Op. 50.
Schicksalslied. Op. 54.
Sapphische Ode. Op. 94, No. 4. (Ilda Tilike.)
Serenade. Op. 11.
Sonate (nach d. Sextett. Op. 18). (Robert Keller.)
Symphonien. Op. 68. 73. 90. 98.
*Ungarische Tänze. Heft 1. 2. S. 150.
 —— Heft 3. 4. (Th. Kirchner.) S. 150.
 —— In erleichterter Spielart. Heft 1—4.
 (Robert Keller.) S. 150.
Variationen. Op. 23. 56.
Walzer. Op. 39.
Wiegenlied. Paraphrase über Op. 49, No. 4.
Zigeunerlieder. Op. 103. (Th. Kirchner.)
Zigeunerlied aus Op. 103, No. 7. (Ilda Tilike.)
4 Zigeunerlieder. Op. 112, No. 3—6.

D. Für Orgel.

Adagio aus Op. 78.
Akademische Fest - Ouvertüre. Op. 80.
Andante grazioso aus Op. 101.
Intermezzi. Op. 116, No. 4. 6. Op. 117, No. 1.
Scherzo aus Op. 11.
Ungarische Tänze. No. 1. 5.
„Wir wandelten, wir zwei —" (Lieder. Op.
 96, No. 2.)

E. Für Harfe.

Wiegenlied. Op. 49, No. 4. (Beatrix Fels.)

F. Für Zither.

Drei Lieder v. Johannes Brahms (mit Gesang
 ad libitum) von Anton Hölzer. (No. 1. Wiegenlied, S. 44. — No. 2. Vergebliches Ständchen, S. 87. — No. 3. Minnelied, S. 76.)

G. Für Gesang.

1) Für Männerchor und Orchester.

Das Lied vom Herrn von Falkenstein. Op. 43,
No. 4. (*Heuberger.*)

2) Für Männerchor ohne Begleitung.

Deutsche Volkslieder. Heft I—IV. (No. 2—6.
8. 10. 13. 17. 19. 22—26. 29—32. 36. 37. 39.
41. 42.) (*Fr. Hegar.*) S. 140.
„Dort in den Weiden“. Op. 97, No. 4.
Trennung. Op. 97, No. 6.
Vergebliches Ständchen. Op. 84, No. 4.
Wiegenlied. Op. 49, No. 4.

3) Für 3 Frauenstimmen mit Pianoforte.

Deutsche Volkslieder. No. 1. 3. 5. 8. 9. 15.
16. 20. 22—24. (*Fr. Hegar.*) S. 140.

4) Für 3 Frauenstimmen ohne Begleitung.

Deutsche Volkslieder. No. 6. (*Fr. Hegar.*)
S. 140.

5) Chorwerke mit Pianoforte.

(Clavierauszüge.)

*Ave Marie. Op. 12.
*Begräbnissgesang. Op. 13.
*Gesang der Parzen. Op. 89.

*Gesänge für Frauenchor. Op. 17.
* —— für 6stimm. Chor. Op. 42.
Das Lied vom Herrn v. Falkenstein. Op. 43,
No. 4.
*Lieder und Romanzen f. Frauenchor. Op. 44.
2 Hefte.
*Motetten. Op. 29, No. 1. 2.
*Nänie. Op. 82.
*Requiem. Op. 45.
*Rhapsodie. Op. 53.
*Rinaldo. Op. 50.
*Schicksalslied. Op. 54.
*Triumphlied. Op. 55.

6) Duette mit Pianoforte.

Zigeunerlied: „Wir leben nur von heut’ auf
morgen.“ (Nach ungarischen Tänzen arrang.
von *Pauline Viardot.*) S. 151.

7) Sologesänge mit Pianoforte.

Ausgewählte Lieder. 7 Bände. S. 133.
Neue Ausgaben für hohe und tiefe Stimme
von Op. 19. 46 bis 49. 69—72.
Transponirte Ausgaben von Op. 3. 7. 32,
No. 9. Op. 33. 43, No. 1. 2. Op. 57—59. 63.
84. 85. 86. 94—97. 103. 105 bis 107. 112,
No. 3—6. 121 und Mondnacht. S. 141.
4 Zigeunerlieder aus Op. 112, No. 3—6.

b) Namen- und Sach-Register.